D1445701

# THE ONLINE CUSTOMER

# THE ONLINE CUSTOMER

## New Data Mining and Marketing Approaches

*Yinghui Yang*

# CAMBRIA
## PRESS

YOUNGSTOWN, NEW YORK

This book has been registered with the Library of Congress.
Yinghui, Yang
        The Online Customer / Yinghui Yang
        p. cm.
        Includes biographical references
        ISBN10:  1-934043-06-0
        ISBN13:  978-1-934043-06-6

*For my mom Caiyu,*
*my husband Tao,*
*and*
*my daughter Diane*

# TABLE OF CONTENTS

# LIST OF TABLES

# LIST OF FIGURES

# FOREWORD

Various business problems such as market segmentation, targeted marketing, personalization, cross selling and modeling customer lifetime value are of interest to both the data mining and marketing academic communities. However, these two disciplines have different approaches to analyzing these problems. Data mining research incorporates methodologies from various disciplines such as statistics, machine learning, databases, optimization and pattern recognition, and is primarily data-driven. It focuses more on the effectiveness of problem solving, and pays greater attention to actual performance on data. In contrast, marketing research advocates more theory-based analysis and its theories are often built upon statistics, psychology, economics and other social sciences. The broader research goal that motivates the ideas described here is to integrate and compare methods from marketing research and data mining research to solve marketing problems.

This book consists of two essays that contribute to this goal. In each essay, data mining and marketing approaches are used to address specific marketing problems. The first essay develops a new data mining method and applies it to a market segmentation problem. At the same time, comparisons are made between the proposed method and commonly used methods from both data mining and marketing research. The results show that the proposed method performs very well. The second essay focuses on a specific marketing problem: the relationship between free shipping promotions and Internet shopping behavior. It uses original analytical models and empirical methods from both marketing and data mining research to address the problem.

Each essay is independently evaluated on different data sets originating from the Web. Researchers and practitioners often struggle with how to best to leverage clickstream data given various idiosyncratic challenges. The use of real Web clickstream data in this research adds another dimension that will be of significant interest.

Building on the notion that observable customer transactions are generated by latent behavioral traits, the first essay investigates the use of a novel pattern-based clustering approach to grouping customer transactions. An objective function is defined and maximized in order to achieve a good clustering of customer transactions. An algorithm groups customer transactions such that patterns generated from each cluster are homogeneous within but heterogeneous between cluster groups. Experimental results from user-centric Web usage data demonstrate that the proposed approach generates a highly effective clustering of transactions. These behavior-based clusters are then used to build more accurate predictive models. A notable strength of the approach is the ability to label the clusters with behavioral patterns and describe the differences between clusters with contrasting behavioral patterns. An important contribution of this first essay is the development of this novel clustering approach that is based on the concept of pattern difference and similarity.

The main contribution of the second essay is that it studies an important Internet marketing problem that has not been well researched. It analyzes the impact of different free-shipping schedules on the shopping behavior of a rational shopper and derives closed-form solutions for various questions. The analysis elegantly characterizes the optimal shopping policy of a rational shopper and examines the difference among different free-shipping schedules. It also empirically tests some hypotheses generated from the theoretical model using purchase data from various Web sites.

In summary, this research is highly recommended for scholars and practitioners who are at the interface of data mining and marketing.

Dr. Balaji Padmanabhan
Assistant Professor of Operations and
Information Management
The Wharton School, University of Pennsylvania

# PREFACE

This research was completed in May 2004 and submitted to University of Pennsylvania as partial fulfillment of requirements for a PhD degree in Operations and Information Management. The first part of the research focuses on using behavior patterns for customer segmentation. It advances data mining theory by presenting a novel pattern-based clustering approach for customer segmentation. The second part of the research studies free-shipping promotions on the Internet. Since May 2004, there have been academic contributions and developments in industry that are especially relevant to this research.

First, Xiong et al. (2005) points out that there has been considerable interest in using association patterns for clustering. Although several interesting algorithms have been developed, further investigation is needed to characterize the benefits of using association patterns and the most effective way of using them for clustering. They present a new clustering technique – bisecting K-means Clustering with pAttern Preservation (K-CAP) – which exploits key properties of the hyperclique association pattern and bisecting $k$-means. Experimental results on document data show that, in terms of entropy, K-CAP can perform substantially better than the standard bisecting $k$-means algorithm when the data sets contain clusters of widely different sizes – the typical situation. Furthermore, because hyperclique patterns can be found much more efficiently than other types of association patterns, K-CAP retains the appealing computational efficiency of bisecting $k$-means.

Jiang et al. (2005) points out that pattern-based clustering has broad applications in microarray data analysis, customer segmentation, e-business data analysis, etc. However, pattern-based clustering often returns a large number of highly-overlapping clusters, which makes it hard for users to identify interesting patterns from the mining results. Moreover, pattern-based clustering lacks a general model. Different kinds of patterns or different measures on the pattern coherence may require different algorithms. They address the above two problems by proposing a general quality-driven approach to mining top-$k$ quality pattern-based clusters. They examine the quality-driven approach using real world microarray data sets. The experimental results show that their method is general, effective and efficient.

Second, scholarly interest in free shipping appears to be increasing, perhaps because scholars have started to realize the importance of free shipping promotions in driving customer shopping behavior on the Internet. From a scholarly perspective, there is one significant paper that has appeared.

Lewis et al. (2006) provides an empirical study on the impact of shipping and handling charges on consumer purchasing behavior. Using a database from an online retailer that has experimented with a wide variety of shipping-fee schedules, they investigate the impact of shipping charges on order incidence and order size. They use an ordered probability model that is generalized to account for the effects of non-linear and discontinuous shipping fees on purchasing decisions, and to accommodate heterogeneity in response parameters. Results show that consumers are very sensitive to shipping charges and that shipping fees influence order incidence and basket size. Promotions such as free shipping and free shipping for orders that exceed some size threshold are found to be very effective in generating additional sales. However, the lost revenues from shipping and the lack of response by several segments are substantial enough to render such promotions unprofitable to the retailer. Heterogeneity across consumers also suggests interesting opportunities for the retailer to customize the shipping and other marketing-mix promotion offerings.

The ongoing interest in pattern-based clustering and free shipping among those in academic and practitioner circles shows, I believe, that these are two important areas of study. I hope that researchers will find this study helpful in their own investigations. Consistent with Cambria Press publishing policies, this work has complete documentation and methodology so that future scholars can build upon this work. However, I also provide a concise Executive Summary for managers who wish to have a quick overview of the complete work and its findings.

## REFERENCES

Michael, L., Singh, V., and Fay, S., 2006. An Empirical Study of the Impact of Nonlinear Shipping and Handling Fees on Purchase Incidence and Expenditure Decisions. *Marketing Science*, 25(1):51-64.

Jiang, D., Pei, J., and Zhang, A., 2005. A General Approach to Mining Quality Pattern-based Clusters from Gene Expression Data. In *Proceedings of the 10th International Conference on Database Systems for Advanced Applications (DASFAA'05)*, Beijing, China, April 18-20, 2005.

Xiong, H., Steinbach, M., Ruslim, A., and Kumar, V., 2005. Characterizing Pattern based Clustering. University of Minnesota, Department of Computer Science and Engineering Technical Report.

# EXECUTIVE SUMMARY

## INTRODUCTION

The broader objective of the research is to study how data mining and marketing approaches can be used to study marketing problems. In particular, we want to integrate and compare methods from marketing research and data mining research. This research consists of two essays that contribute to this goal. In each of the two essays in this research, both data mining and marketing approaches are used to address selected marketing problems. Although the research stops short at integrating both types of approaches on the methodology level, it does combine both approaches in a way to effectively address the problems.

The first essay addresses customer segmentation problems. In this essay we develop new data mining methods and apply them to customer segmentation problems. Other two popular methods from the marketing literature are used in the evaluation step of the essay. In this essay, we want to show how data mining methods can help solve customer segmentation problems in a data rich environment. The second essay focuses on a specific marketing problem: the relationship between free shipping promotions and Internet shopping behavior. It develops original analytical models that generate hypotheses that are tested on Internet data. A data mining method called *contrast set* is used for empirical testing.

## EXISTING LITERATURE

The first essay relates to literature in the fields of market segmentation, pattern-based clustering, segmentation-based modeling, profiling, and signature discovery.

There are hundreds of clustering algorithms and segmentation approaches proposed in the statistics, data mining and marketing literature. There are distance based nonhierarchical clustering algorithms (e.g. *k*-means), hierarchical clustering algorithms (including agglomerative and divisive algorithms), model-based clustering algorithms and various other approaches that are not grouped into any of the above three categories (e.g. rule-based approaches, neural networks). The research that is most related to our method can be categorized into four groups that are now described.

### Market Segmentation

Two dimensions of segmentation research include segmentation bases and methods. A segmentation basis is defined as a set of variables or characteristics used to assign potential customers to homogenous groups. Research in segmentation bases focuses on identifying effective variables for segmentation. Cluster analysis has historically been the most well-known method for market segmentation. Recently, much of the market segmentation literature has focused on the technology of identifying segments from marketing data through the development and application of finite mixture models. Finite mixture models allow customer behavior to be described by an appropriate statistical model with a mixture component. The main advantage of these models is that they enable statistical inference. In general model-based clustering, the data is viewed as coming from a mixture of probability distributions, each representing a different cluster. If we view the patterns representing a cluster as a type of model generating the observable data (with some noise) within that cluster, the spirit of our approach is similar to that of model-based clustering. Although our approach does not allow statistical inference, it can capture more interesting behavioral patterns.

## Pattern-Based Clustering

With pattern-based clustering, data in the same cluster normally should share common patterns. There are numerous pattern-based clustering models due to various definitions of patterns and distance measures. The definition of a pattern could be the correlation between attributes of objects to be clustered. It can also be other commonly used pattern representations in data mining such as itemsets, association rules, sequential patterns, etc. The distance measures used in pattern-based clustering are normally different from the traditional distance measures (e.g. Euclidean distance, Manhattan distance and cosine distance, which are not always adequate in capturing patterns among the objects). Most pattern-based clustering methods only utilize pattern similarity. We incorporate pattern difference and similarity at the same time. We define an objective function that we maximize in order to achieve a good clustering of customer transactions and present a method that groups customer transactions such that patterns represented in itemsets generated from each cluster demonstrate homogeneity within but heterogeneity between representations.

## Segmentation-Based Modeling

In statistics and econometrics, there are various models that split the input space (instead of objects to be clustered) according to the observed input variables, and a regression model is fit in each subspace. Typically, a cut in one of the input variables is introduced, and in each subspace a separate linear model is fit. These models all decide where to split the input space according to the observed input variables. There are several such segmentation-based approaches in market segmentation and it has been established that this tactic can help build better customer models. Clusterwise regression is a method for simultaneous clustering (not using the mixture model) and building predictive models. In a regression context the method clusters subjects nonhierarchically in such a way that the fit of the regression within clusters is optimized.

Under the mixture model framework, mixture regression models simultaneously group subjects into unobserved segments and estimate a regression model within each segment by relating a dependent variable to a set of independent variables. The mixture regression methods represent the mixture analog to the clusterwise regression methods. The identification of segments and simultaneous estimation of the response functions within each segment have been accomplished using a variety of mixture regression models.

At the crossing of the connectionist community and the time series community, Gated Expert models introduce chosen external variables to detect the switching of regimes in time series data. It consists of a gating neural network and several competing neural networks. The gating network learns to predict the probability of the prediction of each expert. The input of the gating network includes chosen external variables which are picked manually. When the driving force behind the splitting of the input space is unknown, it is not guaranteed that the hand-picked external variables will cover the hidden driving factors. In addition, effort needs to be taken to gather information about those external variables possibly for every data point in the training data set. Again, the gated expert method focuses on time series data, while our research emphasizes transaction data. The significant difference between our approach and the above methods is the use of pattern-based clustering approach to learn the individual segments.

*Profiling and Signature Discovery*

In market segmentation research, demographic and socioeconomic variables are often used for profiling purposes. They are used in segmentation studies to profile segments in order to enhance identifiability and accessibility. In this way, segments can be targeted, as media profiles and market areas are often described with demographic variables. In mixture models, profiling of segments is typically performed by using the posterior segment membership probabilities that provide the probability that a particular subject belongs to each of the derived segments. The segments derived from the mixture models have been profiled by most researchers in the second step of the analysis. Several marketing researchers have proposed models that simultaneously profile the derived segments with descriptor variables. In our modeling framework, we incorporate signature discovery techniques. In signature discovery and profiling research within the data mining community, studies have focused primarily on extracting features (variables) and generating rules to represent signatures for an individual customer. Signatures are often used for personalization and fraud detection.

The second essay studies a specific problem. As far as we know, this is the first research to examine free shipping promotions on the Internet in a theoretical framework. Researchers have studied shipping fees before but not specifically issues related to free shipping.

## RESEARCH PROBLEMS AND SOLUTIONS

In the first essay, we study a new approach to segmenting customer transactions that is based on the idea that there may exist natural behavioral patterns in different groups of transactions. In such cases, appropriate "pattern-based clustering" approaches can constitute an intuitive method for grouping customer transactions. At the highest level, the idea is to cluster customer transactions such that patterns generated from each cluster, while similar to each other within the cluster, are very different from the patterns generated from other clusters. Customers' behavioral patterns can have different representations. A behavioral pattern can be represented as an IF-THEN rule. It can be represented by a collection of things (called an "itemset" in the data mining literature) a customer does together. It is also common to use sequences for pattern representation. Correlation between the values of different variables can also be considered as a type of pattern. We suggest that different domains may have different representations for what "patterns" are and for how to define differences between sets of patterns. We investigate the utility of pattern-based clustering for grouping Web transactions. In particular, we argue that itemsets are a natural representation for patterns in Web transactions and present GHIC (Greedy Hierarchical Itemset-based Clustering) – a pattern-based clustering algorithm for domains in which itemsets are the natural pattern representation.

After evaluating GHIC on 80 sub-datasets generated from a Web browsing data set, we further develop a modeling framework for building segment-level predictive models based on the pattern-based clustering approach and signature discovery techniques. Each category/cluster of customer transactions discovered by the pattern-based clustering approach can be characterized by its own distinguishing patterns. After we elicit multiple categories of customer transactions, we build one signature capturing the salient behavioral patterns for each category, as well as one predictive model for each category. In the prediction stage, a new transaction is compared with all the signatures and the closest signature is chosen. Then this new transaction is assigned to the category of transactions that the signature represents and the model associated with this signature is used to predict this transaction (or the models combined using a weighting scheme). Experiments conducted using online purchasing data are used in this study to evaluate the modeling technique and compare the proposed approach with other approaches from data mining and marketing (RFM, GLIMMIX, and *k*-means).

In the second essay, we investigate the problems related to designing a successful shipping-fee policy on the Internet. In this essay, we compare different shipping schedules in terms of how they affect shoppers' purchase behavior. In addition, we investigate the relationship between price and the free-shipping threshold. We first build analytical models to derive closed-form solutions for the questions we want to address. Hypotheses are generated based on the analytical models. We then use Internet shopping data on various Web sites to test the hypotheses. Both marketing methods and data mining methods are utilized in the empirical testing. In the model, we consider 5 different shipping schedules. We formulate the cost that a rational shopper incurs under each shipping schedule, and derive the optimal purchase quantity for the shopper. By comparing the cost associated with each shipping schedule, we are able to draw conclusions about which shipping schedule a shopper will prefer. Furthermore, we investigate the relationship between price and the free-shipping threshold (the total amount a shopper needs to spend in a purchase transaction in order to get free shipping). Our solution suggests that stores with different prices can be equally competitive if they set the right free-shipping threshold level.

# ACKNOWLEDGEMENTS

This book would not have been completed without the help of many individuals. Many thanks to Dr. Balaji Padmanabhan, Dr. Steve Kimbrough, Dr. Thomas Lee, Dr. David Bell, Dr. Skander Essegaier and Dr. Jacob Zahavi for their help in shaping up the materials in this book. I'm very grateful to the staff, especially Ms. Toni Tan at Cambria Press for their editing, formatting and proof reading of the book. I am also thankful for the reviewers of this book. Finally, I thank for my family for their wholehearted support.

# Part I

# Introduction

# 1

# INTRODUCTION

As technology advances, businesses are able to gather an enormous amount of data in their day-to-day operations. This increase in available data has accelerated the adoption of data mining techniques in marketing practice. Acquiring new customers and retaining existing customers is a vital goal of every customer-oriented organization. Toward this end, both data mining and marketing research communities are trying to find solutions to help businesses achieve this goal through marketing strategies such as market segmentation (Kleinberg et al. 1998, Wedel and Kamakura 1998), direct marketing (Pijls et al. 2001, Chiang et al. 2003), targeted marketing (Chauchat et al. 2001, Shaffer and Zhang 1995), personalization/ customization (Goldberg et al. 1992, Ansari et al. 2000, Cooke et al. 2002), market basket analysis/cross selling (Manchanda 1999, Brijs 2000) and customer lifetime value (McDougall 1997, Mani 1999).

The above marketing strategies have always been the subject of study in the field of marketing since they are really at the core of marketing.

Data mining techniques have shown their value in analyzing specific marketing problems in recent years, especially as more and more businesses start to utilize the Internet to conduct business and as data becomes abundant. While the two research communities share the same interests, their methodologies are quite different. For example, in market basket analysis, the data mining literature often focuses on discovering frequently co-purchased items (Agrawal 1995, Brijs 2000); in contrast, marketing researchers tend to build multicategory purchase models based on consumer utility theories (Manchanda 1999), and study the relationship among items, such as their complementarity and/or substitutability. In market segmentation, distance-based clustering techniques, such as $k$-means (Hartigan 1975), and parametric mixture models such as Gaussian mixture models (Fraley and Raftery 1998) represent two main approaches used in marketing research; various algorithm-based clustering techniques are developed in the data mining literature.

In general, data mining research incorporates methodologies from various research communities such as statistics, machine learning, database technology, optimization and pattern recognition, and hence has a richer pool of knowledge/model representation. It focuses more on the effectiveness of problem solving, and pays greater attention to the actual performance on data. On the other hand, marketing research advocates more theory-based analysis and its theories are often built upon statistics, economics, econometrics and other social sciences.

The broader objective of the research is to study how data mining and marketing approaches can be used to study marketing problems. In particular, we want to integrate and compare methods from marketing research and data mining research. This research consists of two essays that contribute to this goal. In each of the two essays in this research, both data mining and marketing approaches are used to address selected marketing problems. Although the research stops short at integrating both types of approaches on the methodology level, it does combine both approaches in a way to effectively address the problems.

TABLE 1. Relationship of the two essays

| Problems / Methods/Models | Data Mining | Marketing |
|---|---|---|
| Customer Segmentation | New method | Evaluation |
| Free-shipping Promotion | Evaluation | New model |

As shown in Table 1, the first essay addresses customer segmentation problems. In this essay we develop new data mining methods and apply them to customer segmentation problems. Other two popular methods from the marketing literature are used in the evaluation step. In this essay, we want to show how data mining methods can help solve customer segmentation problems in a data rich environment.

The second essay focuses on a specific marketing problem: the relationship between free shipping promotions and Internet shopping behavior. It develops original analytical models that generate hypotheses that are tested on the Internet data. A data mining method called *contrast set* is used for empirical testing.

Each essay is independently evaluated on different data sets. These data sets all originate from the Web. While data generated online has been extensively studied in the data mining community and used in marketing practice, the marketing research community has not developed a significant body of research based on such data, due partially to the overwhelming amount of data, noise in the data and effort needed to preprocess the data

In the first essay, we study how data mining concepts such as patterns can be used to help represent the underlying behavior governing the generation of the data and how the flexibility in representation can help us develop more effective methods in discovering segments in the data and build more accurate predictive models. We study a new approach to segmenting customer transactions that is based on the idea that natural behavioral patterns may exist in different groups of transactions. At the highest level, the idea is to cluster customer transactions such that patterns generated from each cluster, while similar to each other within the cluster, are very different from the patterns generated from other clusters. We further develop a modeling framework for building segment-level predictive models based on the pattern-based clustering approach and signature discovery techniques. We evaluate our pattern-based clustering and model-building approach using different experiments involving 90 different datasets generated from the Web. In each experiment, we compare our approach with several segmentation approaches in data mining and marketing.

In the second essay, we develop original analytical models that address issues related to free shipping promotions and Internet shopping behavior. In order to empirically test the hypotheses generated from the models, we use both common marketing approaches and a data mining method.

The contributions of this research are as follows: (1) We develop a novel pattern-based clustering approach and demonstrate the strength of incorporating unique concepts in data mining and data mining techniques to solve marketing problems. (2) We develop a segmentation-based modeling framework based on a pattern-based clustering approach and signature discovery techniques. (3) We develop original analytical models to derive free-shipping policies, and empirically study issues associated with free-shipping promotions for online shopping. (4) By studying two marketing problems using both data mining and marketing methodologies, we provide insights about the value of both research streams in addressing marketing problems.

# Part II

# Segmenting Customer Transactions Using a Pattern-Based Clustering Approach

2

# SEGMENTING CUSTOMER TRANSACTIONS USING A PATTERN-BASED CLUSTERING APPROACH

## 2.1 INTRODUCTION

Businesses gather an enormous amount of data in their day-to-day operations. Every interaction with a customer generates data and the amount of data gathered is rising exponentially (Ericsson 2003). As technology advances, firms are able to track the origin of the transactions through customer identifiers such as cookies, shopper cards, credit card numbers, cell phone numbers etc. More and more, firms are increasingly realizing the importance of understanding and leveraging customer-level data, and critical business decision models are being built upon analyzing such data (Linden et al. 2003). For example, Amazon.com offers distinct home pages and recommends new products for customers based on personalization models built from data. Most credit card and cellular phone fraud alerts are also issued based on analysis of customer-level data (Fawcett and Provost 1997). Consumer brand choice models and pricing models are heavily used in marketing endeavors (Bell and Lattin 2000, Danaher et al. 2003).

While the expectation for customer-level data analysis is high, there are still problems with existing analytical methods. For example, consumers still receive a significant amount of direct mail advertising products for which they have no interest; online recommendations are still far from perfect (Riedl 2001). In order to create more successful personalized systems and build more accurate consumer behavior models, firms must understand their customers better by collecting more information and better analyzing transaction data. There has been much research in this direction, and clustering transactions to discover segments has been one research stream that has generated a variety of useful approaches (Strehl and Ghosh 2000).

In the marketing literature, market segmentation approaches have often been used to divide customers into groups in order to implement different strategies (Hofstede 2002). It has been long established that customers demonstrate heterogeneity in their product preferences and buying behaviors (Allenby and Rossi 1999) and that the model built on the market in aggregate is often less efficient than models built for individual segments. Much of this research focuses on examining how variables such as demographics and socioeconomic status can be used to predict differences in consumption and brand loyalty. Distance-based clustering techniques, such as $k$-means (Hartigan 1975), and parametric mixture models, such as Gaussian mixture models (Fraley and Raftery 1998), are two main approaches used in segmentation. While both of these approaches have produced good results in various applications, there are well-known drawbacks to these methods (Wedel and Kamakura 1998). While distance-based clustering in an $n$ dimensional space is convenient, it is generally not clear why it is the appropriate method for grouping customers or customer transactions. For mixture models, changing model parameters to represent the difference between segments can often oversimplify the differences and can ignore variables and patterns that are not captured by the parametric models.

In this research we study a new approach to segmenting customer transactions that is based on the idea that there may exist natural behavioral patterns in different groups of transactions. For example, a set of behavioral patterns that distinguish a group of wireless subscribers may be as follows:

- Their call duration during weekday mornings is short, and these calls are within the same geographical area.
- They call from outside the home area on weekdays and from the home area on weekends.
- They have several "data" calls on weekdays.

The above set of three patterns may be representative of a group of consultants who travel frequently and who exhibit a set of common behavioral patterns. This example suggests that there may be natural clusters in data characterized by a set of typical behavioral patterns. In such cases, appropriate "pattern-based clustering" approaches can constitute an intuitive method for grouping customer transactions.

At the highest level, the idea is to cluster customer transactions such that patterns generated from each cluster, while similar to each other within the cluster, are very different from the patterns generated from other clusters. Customers' behavioral patterns can have different representations. A behavioral pattern can be represented as an IF-THEN rule. It represents what a customer will do under a certain circumstance. For example, if it is the weekend, customer X will make a call longer than one hour to California using his cell phone. We can also use a collection of things (called an "itemset" in the data mining literature

(Agrawal et al. 1995)) which reflects what a customer does together to represent certain behavioral patterns. For example, such a pattern could be that customer Y visits yahoo.com, google.com and excite.com in the same Web browsing session. It is also common to use sequences for pattern representation. One such example is that customer W visits cnn.com after msn.com. Correlation between the values of different variables can also be considered as a type of pattern. For example, the price of stock A is positively correlated with the price of stock B.

We suggest that different domains may have different representations for what "patterns" are and for how to define differences between sets of patterns. In the above consultant example, rules are an effective representation for patterns generated from the wireless data; however, in a different domain, such as time series data on stock prices, representations for patterns may be based on "shapes" in the time series. It is easy to see that traditional distance-based clustering techniques and mixture models are not well suited to discover clusters for which the fundamental characterization is a set of patterns such as the ones above.

One reason that pattern-based clustering techniques can generate natural clusters from customer transactions is that such transactions often have natural categories *that are not directly observable from the data*. For example, Web transactions may be for work, for entertainment, shopping for self, shopping for gifts, transactions made while in a happy mood and so forth. Although customers obviously do not indicate which situation they are in before starting a transaction, the set of patterns corresponding to transactions in each category will be different. Transactions at work may be quicker and more focused while transactions for entertainment may be long and across a broader set of sites. Hence, grouping transactions such that the patterns generated from each cluster are "very different" from those generated from another cluster may be an effective method to learn the natural categorizations.

This argument suggests the natural evaluation technique that is used in this essay. We combine transactions with a known natural category – Web transactions from different users (without maintaining the user ID) – and examine how well pattern-based clustering functions in separating transactions that belong to the individual users compared with the traditional clustering techniques.

Motivated by the above argument, we investigate the utility of pattern-based clustering for grouping Web transactions. In particular, we argue that itemsets are a natural representation for patterns in Web transactions and present GHIC (Greedy Hierarchical Itemset-based Clustering), a pattern-based clustering algorithm for domains in which itemsets are the natural pattern representation.

After evaluating GHIC on 80 sub-datasets generated from a Web browsing data set, we further develop a modeling framework for building segment-level predictive models based on the pattern-based clustering approach and signature discovery techniques. Each category/cluster of customer transactions discovered by the pattern-based clustering approach can be characterized by its own distinguishing patterns. After we elicit multiple categories of customer transactions, we build one signature capturing the salient behavioral patterns for each category, as well as one predictive model for each category. In the prediction stage, a new transaction is compared with all the signatures, and the closest signature is chosen. Then this new transaction is assigned to the category of transactions for this signature and the model associated with this signature is used to predict this transaction (or the models combined using a weighting scheme). Experiments conducted on online purchasing data are used in this study to evaluate the modeling technique and compare the proposed approach with other approaches from data mining and marketing (RFM, GLIMMIX, and $k$-means).

The rest of this essay is structured as follows. In Section 2.2 we describe the domain and develop an objective function that will be used to generate pattern-based clusters. Section 2.3 describes GHIC, the technique used to generate the clusters. We present the segmentation-based modeling framework in Section 2.4. Experimental results for pattern-based clustering and the modeling framework are presented in Section 2.5. Related work for both pattern-based clustering and segmentation-based modeling is covered in Section 2.6. In Section 2.7 conclusions are presented.

## 2.2 PATTERN-BASED CLUSTERING OF WEB TRANSACTIONS

How pattern-based clustering works will depend on the choice of pattern representation. In this research we focus on clustering Web transactions and argue that itemsets (Agrawal et al. 1995) are a good representation. Hence in Section 2.2.1 we first describe the domain in some detail to motivate the choice of itemsets as the pattern representation scheme. Subsequently in Section 2.2.2 we present the objective function of our pattern-based clustering.

### 2.2.1 Features of Web Transactions

In this essay we consider users' Web transactions as data records containing categorical and numeric attributes created from the raw data consisting of a series of URLs visited. In our experiments we start with real session-level Web browsing data for users (a session contains a list of consecutive hits within a span of 30 minutes) and create 46 features describing the session/transaction. The terms session and transaction are used interchangeably. The specific features are listed in Table 2.

Note that the features include items concerning time (e.g., average time spent per page), quantity (e.g., number of sites visited), and order of pages visited (e.g., first site); these features include both categorical and numeric types. A conjunction of atomic conditions on these attributes is a good representation for common behavioral patterns in the transaction data. For example, {*starting_time* = *morning, average_time_ page* < 2 *minutes, num_categories* = 3, *total_time* < 10 *minutes*} is a behavioral pattern that may capture a user's specific "morning" pattern of Web usage that involves looking at multiple sites (e.g., work email,

TABLE 2.   Features of a Session/Transaction

| Categories | Metric | Definition |
|---|---|---|
| Time-related | Total time | |
| | Average time per page | Total time/# of pages |
| | Average time per site | Total time/# of sites |
| | Average time per category | Total time/# of categories |
| | Starting time | |
| | Starting day | |
| | Most visited site | |
| | Most visited category | |
| Quantity-related | Number of pages | |
| | Number of sites | |
| | Number of categories | |
| | Average # of pages per site | # of pages/# of sites |
| | Average # of sites per categories | # of sites/# of categories |
| Order-related | First site | |
| | Second site | |
| | Last site | |
| | First category | |
| | Second category | |
| | Last category | |
| Others | Whether or not visited a certain category | 0 – no visit |
| | (total 27 categories) | 1 – at least one visit |

Page: individual Web page, each hit is a page; Site: domain name, such as, www.yahoo.com; Category: such as "travel site", "news site" etc.

news, finance) in a focused manner such that the total time spent is low. Another common pattern for this (same) user may be {*starting_time = night, most_visted_category = games*}, reflecting the user's typical behavior at the end of the day. Here, we treat each attribute-value pair as an item (e.g., *starting_time = night*). A set of attribute-value pairs is treated as an itemset (e.g., {*starting_time = night, most_visted_category = games*}). A frequent itemset is an itemset that occurs in a large number of transactions. In order to capture the typical behavioral patterns in Web transactions, we use itemsets as the representation for patterns. In general, we assume that the items in the itemsets can involve both categorical and numeric attributes, as described in the examples above, and that the functions defined below for the clusters are for the general case. However, in the implementation described in Section 4, we collapse the numeric attributes into categories in order to discover frequent itemsets from data using existing algorithms such as *A priori* (Agrawal et al. 1995). Below we describe the objective function of the pattern-based clustering method.

### 2.2.2 Objective Function for Pattern-Based Clustering

Consider a collection of transactions to be clustered $\{T_1, T_2, \ldots, T_n\}$. Each transaction $T_i$ contains a subset of a list of candidate items $\{i_1, i_2, \ldots, i_m\}$. A clustering $C$ is a partition $\{C_1, C_2, \ldots, C_k\}$ of $\{T_1, T_2, \ldots, T_n\}$ and each $C_i$ is a cluster. The goal of this method is to maximize the difference between clusters and the similarity of transactions within clusters. We cluster to maximize a quantity $M$, where $M$ is defined as follows:

$$M(C_1, C_2, \ldots, C_k) = \text{Difference}(C_1, C_2, \ldots, C_k) + \sum_{i=1}^{k} \text{Similarity}(C_i)$$

Here we only give a specific definition for the difference between two clusters. This is sufficient since hierarchical clustering techniques can be used to cluster the transactions repeatedly into two groups in such a way that the process results in clustering the transactions into an arbitrary number of clusters (which is generally desirable because the number of clusters does not have to be specified up front).

Now, we define the difference between two clusters.

**Definition 1** (Difference between two clusters):
*Let $S_{ad}$ = the number of transactions containing pattern $P_a$ in cluster $C_d$. $|C_d|$ is the number of transactions in cluster $C_d$.*

*Let $S(P_a, C_d) = \dfrac{S_{ad}}{|C_d|}$, and $S(P_a, C_d)$ is called the support of pattern $P_a$ in cluster $C_d$. It is the fraction of transactions in cluster $C_d$ that contain pattern $P_a$.*

$$\text{Difference}(C_i, C_j) = \sum_{a=1}^{m} \frac{\left| S(P_a, C_i) - S(P_a, C_j) \right|}{\frac{1}{2} \cdot \left[ S(P_a, C_i) + S(P_a, C_j) \right]}$$

or

$$\text{Difference}(C_i, C_j) = \sum_{a=1}^{m} \frac{\left| \frac{S_{ai}}{|C_i|} - \frac{S_{aj}}{|C_j|} \right|}{\frac{1}{2} \cdot \left( \frac{S_{ai}}{|C_i|} + \frac{S_{aj}}{|C_j|} \right)}$$

For each pattern $P_a$ ($P_a \in \{P_1, P_2, ..., P_m\}$) considered, we calculate the support of this pattern in cluster $C_i$ and the support of the pattern in cluster $C_j$, then compute the relative difference between these two support values and aggregate these relative differences across all patterns. The support of a pattern in a cluster is the proportion of the transactions containing that pattern in the cluster. The intuition behind the definition of difference is that the support of the patterns in one cluster should be different from the support of the patterns in the other cluster if the underlying behavioral patterns are different. Here we use the relative difference between two support values instead of the absolute difference. The reason is that we consider the difference between 3% and 9% greater than the difference between 90% and 96%, even though they have the same absolute difference. The denominator in the definition is the average value of the two support values. In Appendix 1 we show that under certain natural distributional assumptions the difference metric above is maximized when the correct clusters are discovered.

The set of patterns we consider are the frequent patterns in the original data set. Let *FIS* be the set of all frequent itemsets based on the entire transaction data (before any clustering). Specifically, $FIS = \{is_1, is_2, ..., is_p\}$ where $is_i$ is an itemset in *FIS*. Given a clustering, we calculate the support for each itemset in *FIS* for each cluster and use Definition 1 to calculate the difference between the two clusters generated. An itemset in *FIS* is frequent in the entire set of transactions before clustering, but it is not necessarily frequent for each cluster. For example, the support of an itemset may be 50% before clustering. After clustering, the support of this itemset in cluster 1 may be 0% and the support in cluster 2 may be 100%. Then this itemset may become one of the itemsets that particularly distinguishes the two clusters discovered.

Note that in order to ensure that *FIS* contains any itemset that may be large in some arbitrary cluster, we generate *FIS* using a very low minimum support threshold on the entire transaction data. From a computational point of view this process is efficient since it involves the generation of large itemsets only once, as opposed to running a large itemset generation procedure for every partition in the data that is considered.

Next, we define the similarity of the transactions within a cluster, using the support of the itemsets.

**Definition 2** (Intra-cluster similarity):
*Here, the goal of the similarity measure is to capture how similar transactions are within each cluster. The heuristic is that, if transactions are more similar to each other, then they can be assumed to share more patterns. Hence, one approach is to use the number of strong patterns generated as a proxy for the similarity. If itemsets are used to represent patterns, then the number of frequent itemsets in a cluster can be used as a proxy for similarity where:*

Similarity $S(C_i)$ = *the number of frequent itemsets in cluster* $C_i$

In this section we discussed the use of itemsets to represent behavioral patterns embedded in Web transactions and present an objective function to maximize in order to generate the pattern-based clusters.

In the next section we describe *GHIC*, an algorithm for pattern-based clustering.

## 2.3 THE CLUSTERING ALGORITHM

The ideal algorithm will be one that maximizes $M$ (defined in previous section). However, for the objective function defined above, if there are $n$ transactions and two clusters that we are interested in learning, the number of possible clustering schemes to examine is $2^n$. Hence, a heuristic approach is called for.

After we obtain *FIS* using association rule discovery algorithms, as described in Section 2, we convert the initial transactions into the format shown in Table 3, where rows represent transactions to be clustered and columns represent itemsets. A "1" in a cell indicates that a certain transaction contains a certain itemset. We use $T' = \{T'_1, T'_2, \ldots, T'_n\}$ to represent this new transaction set. Instead of clustering the original transactions, we convert the problem into clustering these binary vectors and present a divisive hierarchical algorithm. The entire transaction set is first divided into two clusters. Each cluster is further divided into two clusters if it has more than a predefined number of transactions. This process is repeated until no cluster is big enough to be divided further. In addition to cluster size, we assume that the stopping conditions are user specified and can contain additional criteria such that if a cluster's size is bigger than the threshold but its quality is very good (contains very similar transactions), we can stop dividing that cluster.

TABLE 3.    TRANSACTIONS REPRESENTED IN ITEMSETS

|         | $is_1$ | $is_2$ | ... | $is_p$ |
|---------|--------|--------|-----|--------|
| $T_1$   | 1      | 0      | ... | 0      |
| $T_2$   | 1      | 0      | ... | 1      |
| ...     | ...    | ...    | ... | ...    |
| $T_n$   | 0      | 1      | ... | 0      |

In order to generate balanced clusters, we introduce another component to $M$. Also because each division creates two clusters, the revised $M$ is specified as follows:

$$M(C_1, C_2) = K_1 \cdot D(C_1, C_2) + K_2 \cdot S(C_1) + K_3 \cdot S(C_2) + f_{BALANCE}(N_1, N_2)$$

$K_1$, $K_2$, $K_3$ are user-specified weights used to bring the difference and similarity to relatively compatible scales and can be decided upon according to simulation. For example, in the simulation, the difference component ranges between 1000 and 2000, and the two similarity components range between 100 and 200. If the difference and similarity need to be considered equally, we can set $K_1$ as 1 and set $K_2$ and $K_3$ as 10.

$D(C_1, C_2)$ represents the inter-cluster difference, $S(C_1)$ and $S(C_2)$ are the intra-cluster similarity for cluster-1 and cluster-2 respectively, and $N_1$ and $N_2$ are the number of transactions in cluster-1 and cluster-2 respectively. $f_{BALANCE}(N_1, N_2)$ can take one of the following formats.

$$f_{BALANCE}(N_1, N_2) = -K_4 \cdot |N_1 - N_2| \tag{A}$$

$$f_{BALANCE}(N_1, N_2) = \begin{cases} 0, & K_l \le \dfrac{N_1}{N_2} \le K_h \\[2ex] -\infty, & \dfrac{N_1}{N_2} > K_h \ \text{or} \ \dfrac{N_1}{N_2} < K_l \end{cases} \tag{B}$$

$f_{BALANCE}(N_1, N_2)$ serves as a tool to balance the size of the two clusters generated. It can either be a linear function of the absolute difference between the size of the two clusters (A), or a discrete function of the relative difference of the size of the two clusters (B). In (B), if the size of cluster-1 is very different from the size of cluster-2 (case 2 in (B)), this balancing component of $M$ will drive $M$ to $-\infty$ meaning that this cluster will not be considered. $K_l$ and $K_h$ are the desired lower bound and upper bound of $N_1/N_2$. For a given clustering, if $N_1/N_2$ is out of these two bounds (clusters generated are unbalanced), this clustering will not be considered. *GHIC* is presented in Figure 1.

Global model (no segmentation), *k*-means, the RFM-based (Recency, Frequency and Monetary value) segmentation model and GLIMMIX (Generalized Mixture Regression Model). With RFM, customers can be grouped according to how recently they bought from the retailer, how frequently they bought in a given time period, and how much they spent in that same period. RFM is a popular market segmentation model in the marketing literature and practice (Shepard 1995). Using the site-centric purchasing data we have, we are able to derive values for Recency, Frequency and Monerary value. Customers with the same value for RFM were grouped together. For example, customers with {*Recency = low, Frequency = high, Monetary = high*} were grouped into one segment. For every possible combination of the values of Recency, Frequency and Monerary value, there is a segment. In the prediction stage, a customer is assigned to one of the segments according to the values of the customer's R, F and M. In our experiment, we have three possible values (low, medium, high) for R, F and M. See (Hartigan 1975) for the description of *k*-means and see Appendix 2 for the description of GLIMMIX. Table 4 presents the results comparing the predictive accuracy of the 5 approaches on the hold-out samples.

In our experiment, RFM was not significantly different from the Global model ( $p = 0.3478$ ); GLIMMIX was significantly better than

TABLE 4.   Comparison of Root Mean Squared Errors for Experiment I

|  | Global | RFM | GLIMMIX | *k*-means | GHIC |
|---|---|---|---|---|---|
| amazon.com | 25.07 | 24.68 | 25.24 | 24.28 | 19.36 |
| bestbuy.com | 22.71 | 22.13 | 4.71 | 5.28 | 3.72 |
| bmgmusic.com | 6.61 | 6.67 | 4.94 | 4.58 | 3.30 |
| expedia.com | 35.43 | 36.67 | 26.92 | 27.01 | 26.02 |
| hotwire.com | 24.14 | 32.65 | 11.12 | 17.10 | 13.23 |
| landsend.com | 32.91 | 34.22 | 22.23 | 27.78 | 11.35 |
| orbitz.com | 58.14 | 57.66 | 48.69 | 47.34 | 36.57 |
| qvc.com | 165.63 | 164.31 | 73.63 | 111.10 | 65.58 |
| sears.com | 26.57 | 26.47 | 15.12 | 23.46 | 13.45 |
| ticketmaster.com | 76.95 | 77.46 | 31.33 | 18.90 | 12.48 |

TABLE 5.    Significance of the Comparison (paired *t*-test)

|          | Global | RFM   | GLIMMIX | k-means | GHIC   |
|----------|--------|-------|---------|---------|--------|
| Global   | –      | 0.346 | 0.0206  | 0.0177  | 0.0113 |
| RFM      |        | –     | 0.0162  | 0.013   | 0.0088 |
| GLIMMIX  |        |       | –       | 0.3227  | 0.0096 |
| k-means  |        |       |         | –       | 0.0197 |
| GHIC     |        |       |         |         | –      |

the Global model ( $p$ = 0.0206) and RFM ( $p$ = 0.0162); $k$-means was significantly better than the Global model ( $p$ = 0.0177) and RFM ( $p$ = 0.013), but not significantly different from GLIMMIX ( $p$ = 0.3217); and *GHIC* was significantly better than the Global model ( $p$ = 0.0113), RFM ( $p$ = 0.0088), GLIMMIX ( $p$ = 0.0096) and $k$-means ( $p$ = 0.0197). These results are listed in Table 5. Besides the root mean square error measurement, we also use lift charts (see Figure 3–Figure 12) to assess the performance of the different models. The Lift chart evaluates the benefits of performing a model-based vs. random marketing campaign. The x-axis indicates the percentage of customers selected (1%–5%, 21%–100%), and the y-axis indicates the total profit that the selected customers generate. In 6 out of the 10 data sets, GHIC has the best lift charts (for qvc.com, sears.com, orbitz.com, expedia.com, bmgmusic.com, ticketmaster.com), and for the other 4, it is hard to tell which one is the best. Overall, Global and RFM demonstrate the worse lift charts; GHIC has the best lift charts; and $k$-means and GLIMMIX are in the middle.

### 2.5.2 Experiment II: Evaluating GHIC on User-Centric Web Browsing Sessions

#### 2.5.2.1 Experiment setup

Evaluating whether our grouping of transactions using patterns is "good" is a difficult problem because, like any other clustering technique, it is an unsupervised learning technique. However, as mentioned in the

FIGURE 3.    Lift Chart for amazon.com

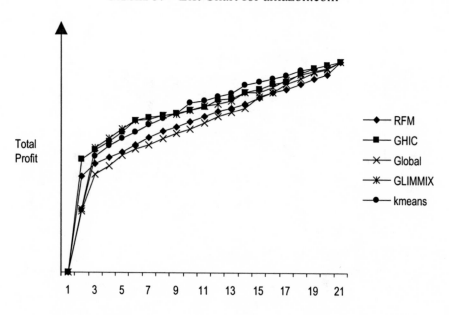

FIGURE 4.    Lift Chart for bestbuy.com

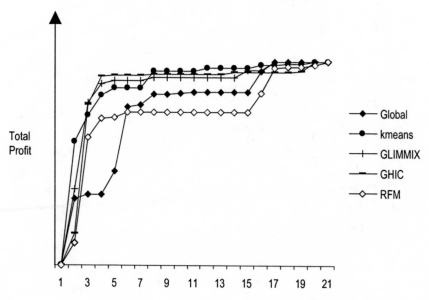

FIGURE 5.    Lift Chart for bmgmusic.com

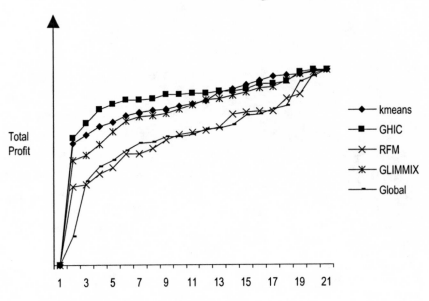

FIGURE 6.    Lift Chart for expedia.com

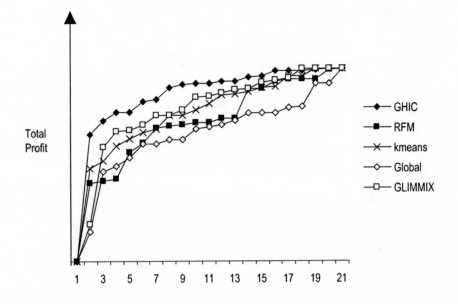

FIGURE 7. Lift Chart for hotwire.com

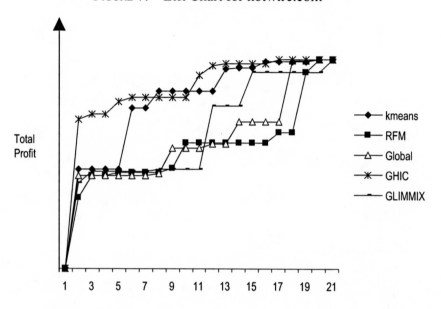

FIGURE 8. Lift Chart for landsend.com

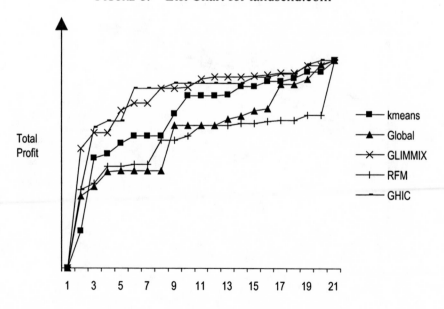

FIGURE 9.    Lift Chart for orbitz.com

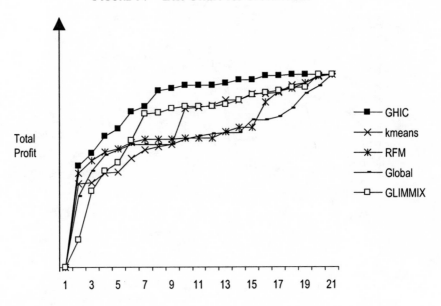

FIGURE 10.    Lift Chart for qvc.com

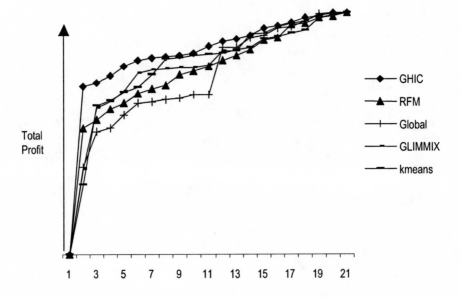

FIGURE 11.    Lift Chart for sears.com

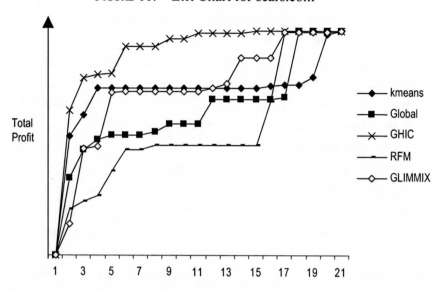

FIGURE 12.    Lift Chart for ticketmaster.com

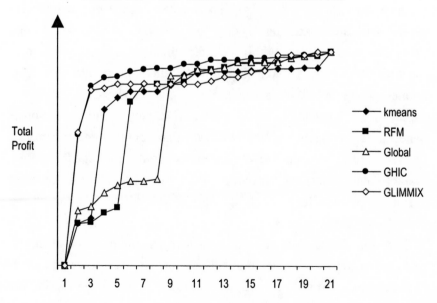

introduction, in order to test the efficacy of pattern-based clustering, we combine transactions with a known category – Web transactions from different users (without maintaining the user ID) – and use entropy to evaluate the distribution of the transactions from different categories in the final clusters. We select the sessions belonging to a certain number of users to form a sub-dataset. In each sub-dataset, each user has relatively the same number of transactions. This can be viewed as if transactions from different categories were randomly distributed in the initial sub-dataset. We wanted to see how the distribution changes after the clustering.

In order to demonstrate the robustness of our approach, we constructed 80 datasets. These datasets were constructed by creating 10 datasets for 8 session types. Session type was classified according to whether the data was for 2, 3, 4, 5, 10, 20, 50, or 100 unique users respectively. The transactions of each user capture that user's online activity over a period of a year. The number of transactions in the 80 datasets varied from 2,000 to 57,000.

In constructing the data, we started with user-centric data provided by a market data vendor. It is important to note that the features listed in Table 2 should be derived from user-centric data, as opposed to site-centric data. Site-centric data is data collected by individual sites about users' accesses to pages within that site; this data is usually stored in log files at each site. Taken individually, site-centric data represents an incomplete picture of user behavior on the Web because it does not capture a user's activity on external sites. User-centric data, on the other hand, is data collected at the user level that captures entire histories of Web surfing behavior for each user. This data is available through market data vendors who provide a randomly chosen subset of users various incentives to permit tracking software to be installed on the client machines.

First, we grouped hits into sessions, using a common rule of thumb that groups consecutive hits within 30 minutes of each other into a session. As described in Section 2, we created 46 features to describe the

TABLE 6.   Transactions Represented in Items

|       | $i_1$ | $i_2$ | ... | $i_p$ |
|-------|-------|-------|-----|-------|
| $T_1$ | 1     | 0     | ... | 1     |
| $T_2$ | 1     | 1     | ... | 0     |
| ...   | ...   | ...   | ... | ...   |
| $T_n$ | 0     | 1     | ... | 1     |

user's behavior for each session. We created an item for each value of the categorical features, categorized the continuous variables according to their value distribution (uniformly binned), and created an item for each bin. After this itemization, we created a session (transaction)-by-item matrix (Table 6) with binary values for each sub-dataset. A "1" in a cell indicates that a certain transaction contains a certain item. $T_1, T_2, \ldots, T_n$ correspond to the sessions in a sub-dataset. Depending on the sub-dataset, there are approximately 2,000 to 10,000 items for each sub-dataset.

From this matrix, we used *A priori* to discover the candidate itemsets and created a matrix like the one in Table 3, to be used as the input to *GHIC*. In the experiment, we set minimum support for *A priori* to discover frequent itemsets to 5%. There were 1,000 to 3,000 itemsets (we restricted these to have a maximum of 3 items) for different sub-datasets.

In order to compare the performance of *GHIC*, we implemented three methods: (1) Hierarchical *k*-means on data represented in items as in Table 6 (the "*k*-means-items" approach), (2) Hierarchical *k*-means on data represented in itemsets as in Table 3 (the "*k*-means-itemsets" approach), and (3) *GHIC* on data represented in itemsets as in Table 3 (the "*GHIC*-itemsets" approach). Hierarchical *k*-means is described in Figure 13. The comparison between *k*-means-items and *k*-means-itemsets can evaluate whether the itemset pattern representation is good, since the two approaches share the same clustering algorithm but are applied on different data formats. The comparison between *k*-means-itemsets and

FIGURE 13.    Hierarchical *k*-means

**Input:**          $C = \{C_0\}$
$C_0 = \{T_1, T_2, \ldots, T_n\}$ – the converted transaction set to be clustered (the transactions can take the forms both as that in Table 6 ("*k*-means-items" approach) and that in Table 3 ("*k*-means-itemsets" approach).
**Output:** Clusters $C = \{C_1, C_2, \ldots, C_l\}$
**Repeat {**
Choose any cluster $X = \{T_1, T_2, \ldots, T_s\}$ from $C$ such that the stopping condition is not satisfied for $X$;
Use *k*-means to cluster $X$ into 2 clusters $C_1$ and $C_2$;
$C = (C - X) \cup C_1 \cup C_2$;
**} While the stopping condition is not satisfied for every $X$ in $C$**

*GHIC* can show whether our algorithm is more effective in clustering data represented in itemsets, since the two use the same data format but different algorithms.

The hierarchical *k*-means algorithm is a divisive hierarchical algorithm that iteratively divides the transactions into two clusters (also known as a type of bisecting *k*-means which is shown to be more effective than the traditional *k*-means (Steinbach et al. 2000)). For each division, we use traditional *k*-means to divide the data into two clusters. The *k*-means algorithm used here is the Euclidean-based *k*-means (Hartigan 1975). The reason for using hierarchical *k*-means is that the number of natural clusters is not known in advance. This is particularly useful because, even for a sub-dataset containing transactions from 2 users, we expect more than 2 clusters, since each user may have more than one set of behavior patterns. If we use just *k*-means instead of hierarchical *k*-means, we get inferior results. For example, when we applied *k*-means on a 2-user dataset, each resulting cluster contained approximately 50% of the transactions from each user. Another reason is that hierarchical *k*-means has the same structure as our pattern-based clustering approach, so we can draw better comparisons between the two.

When we cluster using *GHIC*, we set the values of $K_1$, $K_2$ and $K_3$ to bring the first three components of $M$ to relatively compatible scales. We use (B) as the balancing function. If the size of the smaller cluster is at least 10% of the larger cluster, the value of $f_{BALANCE}(N_1, N_2)$ is 0, and otherwise $-\infty$. This can be implemented in a way that we consider only divisions that generate reasonably sized clusters. The support threshold that we used to define large itemsets for calculating similarity is set to be 20% (we would like this itemset to be very common in a cluster). We have the same value for these parameters throughout the entire experiment. We consider only itemsets that contain fewer than 4 items for computational reasons, and the stopping criterion is that the size of the cluster is smaller than 5% of the size of the dataset to be clustered.

When evaluating the clustering algorithm, two measures of cluster quality are often used (Steinbach et al. 2000). One type of measure allows us to compare different sets of clusters without reference to external knowledge and is called an *internal quality measure*. The other type of measure assesses how well the clustering works by comparing the groups produced by the clustering techniques to known classes. This type of measure is called an *external quality measure*. One popular external measure is entropy (Shannon 1948).

An entropy value is calculated for each cluster generated. The average of all the entropy values is used as a measure of the quality of the clustering. The smaller the entropy value, the better the quality of the clusters. Let $n_h^{(f)}$ denote the number of transactions belonging to customer $f$ in cluster $h$, $n_h$ denote the number of transactions in cluster $h$, $N$ denote the number of clusters generated, and $C_U$ denote the number of users (classes) in the initial sub-dataset. The entropy measurement used to measure the quality of the clustering is as follows:

$$E = -\frac{1}{N} \cdot \sum_{h=1}^{N} \sum_{f=1}^{C_U} \frac{n_h^{(f)}}{n_h} \cdot \log_{C_U}\left(\frac{n_h^{(f)}}{n_h}\right)$$

### 2.5.2.2 Results

Table 7 presents the results on the 80 datasets. Based on a paired *t*-test across all the sub-datasets, *GHIC* significantly outperformed *k*-means-itemsets ($p = 0.0004$), which in turn outperformed *k*-means-items

TABLE 7. Clustering Results for Experiment II

|  | 2-user | 3-user | 4-user | 5-user | 10-user | 20-user | 50-user | 100-user |
|---|---|---|---|---|---|---|---|---|
| k-means-item | 0.28 | 0.49 | 0.57 | 0.59 | 0.84 | 0.88 | 0.90 | 0.93 |
| k-means-itemset | 0.20 | 0.45 | 0.53 | 0.57 | 0.77 | 0.88 | 0.89 | 0.91 |
| GHIC | 0.17 | 0.28 | 0.34 | 0.41 | 0.62 | 0.73 | 0.80 | 0.87 |

($p = 0.004$). Clearly, *GHIC* significantly outperformed $k$-means-items ($p = 0.0001$). The comparison between $k$-means-items and $k$-means-itemsets demonstrated that our itemset pattern representation is good. The comparison between $k$-means-itemsets and *GHIC* showed that our algorithm is more effective in clustering data represented in itemsets. On average, *GHIC* outperformed $k$-means-itemsets by 21% and $k$-means-items by 27%. These significant numbers suggest that pattern-based clustering techniques may be a natural approach to cluster customer transactions such as Web transactions considered in this research.

In addition to the quantitative results, there are several examples of interesting clusters discovered in the data. For example:

- A cluster characterized with weekend behavioral patterns: {*starting_day = Saturday, most_visited_category = sports*} and {*starting_day = Sunday, most_visited_category = services such as chat rooms*} are two significant patterns in this cluster.
- A cluster characterized with entertainment activities in the evening: {*total_time = long, most_visited_category = entertainment, time = evening*} and {*average_time_ per_site = long, most_visited_ category = games, time = evening*} are two significant patterns in this cluster.
- A different cluster with more work-related activities: {*first_ site = hotmail, most_visited_cat = news, average_time_ per_ page = short*} is a significant itemset in this cluster.
- A cluster with shopping patterns driven by Web searches rather than going to favorite sites to make purchases: {*start category = search,*

*most visited category = retail}* is a highly significant itemset in this cluster.

- Two most significant itemsets in one of the clusters were: (1) *{portal_category = yes, first_site = iwon.com}* with support 100% – in contrast, the support for this itemset over the entire dataset was just 9.5%; (2) *{last_category = portal, average_site_per_category = 1}* with support 66.1% – again, in contrast the support over the entire dataset was just 5.7%. Both of these itemsets are reflective of a behavior that is more complex.

In general, the itemsets in some of the clusters suggest highly explainable behavior patterns (as in the first four examples above), while in other cases it is more difficult to place a single behavior type (the fifth example) based on the itemsets in the cluster. This may be in part due to the fact that consumer behavior in the real world is highly complex. In such cases, the clusters generated can still be useful by providing a starting point for deeper understanding of consumer behavior.

Rather than just describing each cluster based on the patterns, an advantage of our method is that we can easily compare two clusters and identify the differences between them. In order to do this systematically we picked every partition generated at some level in the tree and identified the top ten patterns based on support within each cluster and also the top ten patterns that contribute the greatest to the difference metric. Tables 7 and 8 contain two examples of partitions that suggest that our approach can yield good explanations and key insights into what the main differentiating factors are.

Table 8 clearly represents an entertainment cluster and a Portal/ Services/Sports/Corporate cluster. Cluster 1 mainly involves entertainment-related activities. Cluster 2 has more mixed activities involving multiple categories. The patterns that differentiate these two clusters the most are the strong patterns from Cluster 1 although there are also strong patterns

TABLE 8.    The Entertainment Effect

| Top Patterns |
| --- |

| | |
| --- | --- |
| **Cluster 1** | Entertainment = yes (Support: 100%) |
| | Most_visited_cat = Entertainment  (Support: 100%) |
| | Most_visited_cat = Entertainment, Entertainment = yes  (Support: 100%) |
| | Portals = yes  (Support: 82%) |
| | Entertainment = yes, Portals = yes  (Support: 82%) |
| | Most_visited_cat = Entertainment, Portals = yes  (Support: 82%) |
| | Most_visited_cat = Entertainment, Entertainment = yes, Portals = yes  (Support: 83%) |
| | Services = yes  (Support: 64%) |
| | Entertainment = yes, Services = yes  (Support: 64%) |
| | Most_visited_cat = Entertainment, Services = yes  (Support: 64%) |
| | Most_visited_cat = Entertainment, Entertainment = yes, Services = yes  (Support: 64%) |
| **Cluster 2** | Portals = yes  (Support: 83%) |
| | Services = yes  (Support: 77%) |
| | Services = yes, Portals = yes  (Support: 68%) |
| | Sports = yes  (Support: 60%) |
| | Sports = yes, Portals = yes  (Support: 58%) |
| | Services = yes, Sports = yes  (Support: 54%) |
| | Services = yes, Sports = yes, Portals = yes  (Support: 53%) |
| | Corporate = yes  (Support: 51%) |
| | Services = yes, Corporate = yes  (Support: 45%) |
| | Portals = yes, Corporate = yes  (Support: 45%) |
| **Most different Patterns** | Most_visited_cat = Entertainment, Entertainment = yes  (Support Difference: 100%) |
| | Most_visited_cat = Entertainment, (Support Difference: 100%) |
| | Most_visited_cat = Entertainment, Portals = yes  (Support Difference: 82%) |
| | Most_visited_cat = Entertainment, Entertainment = yes, Portals = yes  (Support Difference: 82%) |
| | Entertainment = yes  (Support Difference: 71%) |
| | Most_visited_cat = Entertainment, Services = yes  (Support Difference: 64%) |
| | Most_visited_cat = Entertainment, Entertainment = yes, Services = yes  (Support Difference: 64%) |
| | Sports = yes  (Support Difference: 57%) |
| | Most_visited_cat = Entertainment, Last_cat = Entertainment (Support Difference: 57%) |
| | Most_visited_cat = Entertainment, Last_cat= Entertainment, Entertainment = yes (Support Difference: 57%) |
| | Entertainment = yes, Portals = yes  (Support Difference: 57%) |

*Note:* If there are more than 10 patterns, it means that the ones after the 10th have the same support value as the 10th. Services, Portals, Sports, Corporate and Entertainment are the different Web site categories. Services category includes Web sites such as emails, E-cards, Coupons, Discussion/Chat, etc. Most_visited_cat stands for the most visited category in a Web browsing session. Last_cat stands for the last category in a Web browsing session. Services = yes means that a Web browsing session contains Web sites from the Services category.

from Cluster 2 (e.g. Sports = yes) that contribute to the differences. At a high level it is quite simple to explain what the clustering obtained here is, and this is a major advantage of pattern-based clustering for business applications.

In Table 9, the two clusters are distinguished mainly based on the first and the last category of the Web browsing session. Cluster 1 includes Portal specific activities. The Web sessions in Cluster 1 start from a Portal site and also end with a Portal site. The Web sessions in Cluster 2 are not only related to portal sites, but also to many unclassified sites. The average number of sites per category is low, indicating a broad browsing pattern. Unlike the partition in Table 8, this is something that may be much harder to have guessed *a priori*, but suggests that there may be interesting behavioral signatures in the data corresponding to how people browse (i.e. starting and ending with a portal).

Computationally *GHIC* is linear in the number of transactions to be clustered and linear in the number of itemsets. Since the number of frequent itemsets stays within a certain range (because people can have only a limited number of behavioral patterns), the execution time of *GHIC* is linear to the number of transactions in the dataset (see Figure 14).

## 2.6 LITERATURE REVIEW

There are hundreds of clustering algorithms and segmentation approaches proposed in the statistics, data mining and marketing literature. There are distance based nonhierarchical clustering algorithms (e.g. *k*-means), hierarchical clustering algorithms (including agglomerative and divisive algorithms), model-based clustering algorithms and various other approaches that are not grouped into any of the above three categories (e.g. rule-based approaches, neural networks). Past research that is most related to our approach is now discussed.

### TABLE 9.    The Portal Effect

| **Top Patterns** |
| --- |

| | |
| --- | --- |
| **Cluster 1** | First_cat = Portals  (Support: 100%) |
| | Last_cat = Portals  (Support: 100%) |
| | Portals = yes  (Support: 100%) |
| | Last_cat = Portals, First_cat = Portals  (Support: 100%) |
| | Portals = yes, First_cat = Portals  (Support: 100%) |
| | Portals = yes, Last_cat = Portals  (Support: 100%) |
| | Portals = yes, Last_cat = Portals, First_cat = Portals  (Support: 100%) |
| | Most_visited_cat = Portals  (Support: 72%) |
| | First_cat = Portals, Most_visited_cat = Portals  (Support: 72%) |
| | Last_cat = Portals, Most_visited_cat = Portals  (Support: 72%) |
| | Last_cat = Portals, First_cat = Portals, Most_visited_cat = Portals  (Support: 72%) |
| | Portals = yes, Most_visited_cat = Portals  (Support: 72%) |
| | Portals = yes, First_cat = Portals, Most_visited_cat = Portals  (Support: 72%) |
| | Portals = yes, Last_cat = Portals, Most_visited_cat = Portals  (Support: 72%) |
| **Cluster 2** | Portals = yes  (Support: 79%) |
| | Corporate = yes  (Support: 61%) |
| | Miscellaneous_categories = yes  (Support: 60%) |
| | Portals = yes, Corporate = yes  (Support: 51%) |
| | Portals = yes, Miscellaneous_categories = yes (Support: 50%) |
| | Avg_#_of_sites_per_cat = 1 (of 10 levels) (Support: 50%) |
| | Avg_#_of_sites_per_cat = 2 (of 10 levels) (Support: 40%) |
| | Miscellaneous _categories = yes, Corporate = yes (Support: 39%) |
| | First_cat = Portals  (Support: 36%) |
| | Portals = yes, First_cat = Portals  (Support: 36%) |
| **Most different Patterns** | Last_cat = Portals, First_cat = Portals  (Support Difference: 100%) |
| | Portals = yes, Last_cat = Portals, First_cat = Portals  (Support Difference: 100%) |
| | Last_cat = Portals  (Support Difference: 82%) |
| | Portals = yes, Last_cat = Portals  (Support Difference: 82%) |
| | Last_cat = Portals, First_cat = Portals, Most_visited_cat = Portals (Support Difference: 72%) |
| | First_cat = Portals  (Support Difference: 64%) |
| | Portals = yes, First_cat = Portals  (Support Difference: 64%) |
| | Last_cat = Portals, Most_visited_cat = Portals  (Support Difference: 63%) |
| | Portals = yes, Last_cat = Portals, Most_visited_cat = Portals  (Support Difference: 63%) |
| | Last_site = yahoo.com, First_cat = Portals  (Support Difference: 58%) |
| | Last_site = yahoo.com, Last_cat = Portals, First_cat = Portals (Support Difference: 58%) |
| | Last_site = yahoo.com, Portals = yes, First_cat = Portals  (Support Difference: 58%) |

Note: First_cat stands for the first category of a Web browsing session.  Avg_#_of_sites_per_cat stands for the average number of pages from a category in a Web browsing session. Miscellaneous_categories indicates all the unrecognized Web sites that are not grouped into any category.

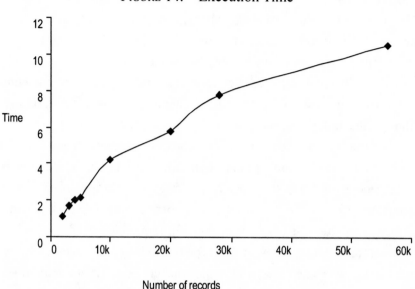

FIGURE 14.   Execution Time

Number of records

## 2.6.1 Market Segmentation

Since the concept emerged in the late 1950s, segmentation has been one of the most researched topics in the marketing literature. There have been two dimensions of segmentation research: segmentation bases and methods. A segmentation basis is defined as a set of variables or characteristics used to assign potential customers to homogenous groups. Research in segmentation bases focuses on identifying effective variables for segmentation, such as socioeconomic status, loyalty, and price elasticity (Frank et al. 1972). Cluster analysis has historically been the most well-known method for market segmentation (Gordon 1980). Recently, much of market segmentation literature has focused on the technology of identifying segments from marketing data through the development and application of finite mixture models (see Böhning (1995) for a review). Finite mixture models are model based and allow customer behavior to be described by an appropriate statistical model with a mixture component. The main advantage of these models is that they enable statistical inference. However, the main drawbacks of these models are: (1) The models are mostly evaluated based on statistical fit; (2) the optimum reached from a particular start may not be the global optimum; (3) the model can simplify the differences between clusters, ignore other attributes not in the hypothesized distribution, and ignore patterns across attributes; and (4) the independence assumption may not be valid on real data (e.g., in the Web browsing situation, many variables, such as total time spent and the total number of pages visited, are highly interdependent).

In general model-based clustering (Fraley and Raftery 1998, Fraley and Raftery 2002), the data is viewed as coming from a mixture of probability distributions, each representing a different cluster. If we view the patterns representing a cluster as a type of model generating the observable data (with some noise) within that cluster, the spirit of our approach is similar to that of model-based clustering. Although our approach does not allow statistical inference, it can capture more interesting behavioral patterns.

### 2.6.2 Pattern-Based Clustering

Wang et al. (2002) consider two objects to be similar if they exhibit a coherent pattern on a subset of dimensions. Their definition of a pattern is based on the correlation between attributes of objects to be clustered. They then use pattern similarity to measure the distance between two objects. They point out that the traditional distance measures (e.g. Euclidean distance, Manhattan distance and cosine distance) are not always adequate in capturing correlations among the objects. Strong correlations may still exist among a set of objects even if they are far apart from each other as measured by the traditional distance functions. This definition is fundamentally different from ours. Their pattern similarity is defined between two objects whereas our pattern similarity is defined within a cluster. Ours is more of a "global" type of definition while theirs is pairwise. We incorporate pattern difference and similarity in our clustering; they only utilize pattern similarity. In addition, the specific definition of a pattern used in Wang et al. (2002) makes it suitable for numerical data only.

Pei et al. (2003) built on the research of Wang et al. (2002) and studied the same problem. They provide a more efficient algorithm by discovering only the maximal pattern-based clustering. The idea is to report only those non-redundant pattern-based clusters, and skip trivial sub-clusters. This way the number of clusters can be reduced substantially. They present a more efficient and scalable mining algorithm for the problem defined in Wang et al. (2002).

The pattern-based clustering problem defined in Wang et al. (2002) and Pei et al. (2003) is different from our problem. Their approach is more related to subspace clustering. Some recent studies (Aggarwal et al. 1999, Aggarwal and Yu 2000, Agrawal et al. 1998, Cheng et al. 1999) focused on mining clusters embedded in some subspaces. For example, CLIQUE (Agrawal et al. 1998) is a density and grid based method. It divides data into hyper-rectangular cells and uses the dense cells to construct subclusters. Subspace clustering can be used to semantically compress data. Jagadish et al. (1999) used a randomized algorithm to find fascicles, the subsets of data that share similar values in some attributes.

Wang et al. (2002) is a generalization of subspace clustering. It does not consider exact match, but the correlation of the values in a subspace. A transaction database can be modeled as a binary matrix, where columns and rows stand for items and transactions. "1" in a cell indicates that a certain transaction contains a certain item. Under this representation, the problem of mining frequent itemsets can also be treated as finding dense sub-matrixes.

### 2.6.3 Item/Itemset/Rule-Based Clustering

This essay uses a set of itemsets as the representation of patterns in each cluster. Hence, within the clustering methods dealing with categorical data, those using the concept of large items/itemsets and association rules are particularly relevant. Han et al. (1997) address the problem of clustering-related customer transactions in a market basket database. Frequent itemsets used to generate association rules are employed to construct a weighted hypergraph. Each frequent itemset is a hyperedge in the weighted hypergraph, and the weight of the hyperedge is computed as the average of the confidences for all possible association rules that can be generated from the itemset. Then, a hypergraph partitioning algorithm from Karypis et al. (1997) is used to partition the items such that the sum of the weights of hyperedges that are cut due to the partitioning is minimized. The result is a clustering of items (not transactions) that occur together in the transactions. Finally, the item clusters are used as the description of the cluster and a scoring metric is used to assign customer transactions to the best item cluster. The approach in Han et al. (1997) makes the assumption that itemsets that define clusters are disjoint and have no overlap among them. This may not be true in practice, since transactions in different clusters may have a few common items. Although items are used in their clustering process, it is evident that our approach works fundamentally differently.

Wang et al. (1999) introduce a clustering criterion suggesting that there should be many large items within a cluster and little overlapping of such items across clusters. They then use this criterion to search for a good clustering solution. Wang et al. (1999) also point out that, for transaction data, methods using pairwise similarity, such as $k$-means, have problems in forming a meaningful cluster. For transactions that come naturally in a collection of items, it is more meaningful to use item/rule-based methods.

Yang et al. (2002) address a similar problem as that in Wang et al. (1999), and our work is most similar to LargeItem (Wang et al. 1999) and CLOPE (Yang et al. 2002) in that we do not use any pairwise distance function. We define a global goal and use this goal to guide the clustering process. Compared to LargeItem and CLOPE, our method takes a new perspective of associating itemsets with behavior patterns and using that concept to guide the clustering process. Using this approach, we are able to identify the distinguishing itemsets that represent a cluster of transactions. As noted previously in this essay behavioral patterns describing a cluster are represented by a *set* of itemsets (for example, a set of two itemsets {*weekend, second site = eonline.com*} and {*weekday, second site = cnbc.com*}. We allow the possibility of finding a *set of itemsets* to describe a cluster instead of just a set of items, which is the focus of other item/itemsets-related work. This is important for clustering Web transaction data. We also illustrate in the essay how we cluster Web transaction data with both numeric data and categorical data. Note that the algorithms presented in Wang et al. (1999) and Yang et al. (2002) are very sensitive to the initial seeds that they pick, while our clustering results are stable. Wang et al. (1999) and Yang et al. (2002) do not use the concept of pattern difference and similarity.

On a different note, document clustering methods also use the concept of *terms* (similar to items) for clustering. Beil et al. (2002) introduced an approach that uses frequent item (term) sets for text clustering. Such frequent sets can be discovered using algorithms for association rule mining. To cluster based on frequent term sets, they measure the mutual overlap of frequent sets with respect to the sets of supporting documents. They then present two algorithms for frequent term-based text clustering. One creates flat clustering and the other one creates hierarchical clustering. Their methods also provide an understandable description of the discovered clusters by their frequent term sets. They also point out that most text clustering algorithms rely on the so-called vector-space model (see Zhao and Karypis (2002) for some common approaches in text clustering). They also state that most of the methods of text clustering algorithms do not really address the special challenges of text clustering: they cluster the full high-dimensional vector-space and the centroids/means of the discovered clusters do not provide an understandable description of the clusters. This has motivated the development of new special text clustering methods which are not based on the vector space model. SuffixTree Clustering (Zamir and Etzioni 1998) is a first method following this approach and forms clusters of documents sharing common terms or phrases. Basic clusters are sets of documents containing a single given term. A cluster graph is built with nodes representing basic clusters and edges representing an overlap of at least 50% between the two associated basic clusters. A cluster is defined as a connected component in this cluster graph. The drawback of SuffixTree as pointed out in Beil et al. (2002) is that while two directly neighboring basic clusters in the graph must be similar, two distant nodes (basic clusters) within a connected component do not have to be similar at all. Beil et al. (2002) also argue that a frequent item-based approach of clustering is promising because it provides a natural way of reducing the large dimensionality of the document vector space. Most of these approaches do not define global goals for clustering and, similar to Wang et al. (1999) and Yang et al. (2002), do not discover a set of itemsets.

### 2.6.4 Segmentation-Based Modeling

In statistics and econometrics, there are various models that split the input space (instead of objects to be clustered) according to the observed input variables, and a regression model is fit in each sub-space. Two of the first examples of this idea are the piecewise linear functions (Imai and Iri 1986) and the threshold autoregressive (TAR) model (Tong and Lim 1980). Their splits are very simple. Typically, a cut in one of the input variables is introduced, and in each subspace a separate linear model is fit. More recently, Friedman (1991) has proposed a more flexible model called Multivariate Adaptive Regression Splines (MARS). Piecewise linear functions such as TAR and MARS models all decide where to split the input space according to the observed input variables. This is a problem if the states which drive the splitting are not directly observable. In addition, these methods build regression models for time series data while our approach allows for more flexible selection of local models for transaction data.

As mentioned earlier, there are several such segmentation-based approaches in market segmentation (see Allenby and Rossi (1999) for a review) and it has been established that this tactic can help build better customer models. Clusterwise regression (originally proposed by Späth (1979, 1981, 1982)) is a method for simultaneous clustering (not using mixture model) and building predictive models. In a regression context the method clusters subjects nonhierarchically in such a way that the fit of the regression within clusters is optimized. Under the mixture model framework, mixture regression models (Wedel and DeSarbo 1994) simultaneously group subjects into unobserved segments and estimate a regression model within each segment, relating a dependent variable to a set of independent variables. The mixture regression methods represent the mixture analog to the clusterwise regression methods. The identification of segments and simultaneous estimation of the response functions within each segment have been accomplished by a variety of mixture regression models, including mixtures of linear regressions (DeSarbo and Cron 1988), multinomial logits (Kamakura and Russell 1989), rank logits (Kamakura et al. 1994), Poisson regressions (Wedel et al. 1995, Wedel and DeSarbo 1995), nested logits (Kamakura et al. 1996), and so on.

At the intersection of the connectionist community and the time series community, Gated Expert models (Weigend et al. 1995) introduce chosen external variables to detect the switching of regimes in time series data. It consists of a gating neural network and several competing neural networks. The gating network learns to predict the probability of the prediction of each expert. The input of the gating network includes chosen external variables which are picked manually. When the driving force behind the splitting of the input space is unknown, it is not guaranteed that the hand-picked external variables will cover the hidden driving factors. In addition, effort needs to be taken to gather information about those external variables possibly for every data point in the training data set. Again, the gated expert method focuses on time series data while our research emphasizes transaction data.

## 2.6.5 Profiling and Signature Discovery

In market segmentation research, demographic and socioeconomic variables are often used for profiling purposes. They are used in segmentation studies to profile segments in order to enhance identifiability and accessibility. In this way, segments can be targeted since media profiles and market areas are often described along demographic variables. In mixture models, the profiling of segments is typically performed by using the posterior segment membership probabilities that provide the probability that a particular subject belongs to each of the derived segments (Wedel and DeSarbo 1994). The segments derived from the mixture models have been profiled by most authors in the second step of the analysis. Several authors in marketing have proposed models that simultaneously profile the derived segments with descriptor variables (Dillon, Kumar and de Borrero 1993, Gupta and Chintagunta 1994, Kamakura, Wedel and Agrawal 1994).

In our modeling framework, we incorporate signature discovery techniques. In signature discovery and profiling research within the data mining community, studies have focused on extracting features (variables) (Cortes et al. 2000) and generating rules (Adomavicius and Tuzhilin 2001, Fawcett and Provost 1997) to represent signatures for an individual customer. Signatures are often used for personalization (Adomavicius and Tuzhilin 2001) and fraud detection (Bolton and Hand 2001, Chan et al. 1999, Cortes et al. 2000).

## 2.7 CONCLUSION: CONTRIBUTIONS, LIMITATIONS AND FUTURE WORK

As mentioned in the introduction, the existence of natural categories of customer behavior is intuitive, and these categories influence the transactions observed. We suggest that pattern-based clustering techniques, such as the one described in this research, may be effective in learning such natural categories and can enable firms to understand their customers better and build more accurate customer models. In this research we presented a new approach, *GHIC*, for pattern-based clustering of Web transactions and demonstrated that the technique performs effectively compared with traditional techniques. A notable strength of our approach is the ability to label the clusters with behavioral patterns and describe the differences between clusters according to contrasting behavioral patterns as our experiments demonstrate.

While the approach developed in this research is promising, we do observe some limitations of the work. (1) As the empirical work demonstrates, some segmentation approaches perform better for certain data sets, but not others. We conducted extensive experiments to investigate the performance of different approaches, but we are unable to identify the factors affecting the performance. Future research should investigate such factors. This may involve manipulating synthetic data sets, controlling different sets of parameters of the segmentation approaches, and/or conducting deeper computational analysis. (2) In this research we provide a heuristic-based algorithm for pattern-based clustering and empirically demonstrate that the algorithm is effective, but we do not study how close to optimal the solution is. (3) The comparison conducted in the research is among several chosen approaches. A wider selection, especially selecting an item/itemset/rule base is desirable. (4) Using more types of data sets to further test the performance of various approaches should also provide more insights.

We plan to extend this research along the following directions. (1) In this research, we use itemsets to represent patterns and develop associated objective functions and algorithm for such representations. As pointed out earlier, the method can be extended to different pattern representations, such as rules and sequences. (2) The method also has the potential to refine the objective function and algorithm for different applications (e.g. DNA sequence analysis, text clustering, stock clustering, etc.), since applications have different domains of knowledge that can facilitate the development of more effective methods.

# Part III

## Free Shipping Promotions and Internet Shopping Behavior: Theory and Evidence

we investigate the relationship between price and the free shipping threshold. We first build analytical models to derive closed-form solutions for the questions we want to address. Hypotheses are generated based on the analytical models. We then use Internet shopping data on various Web sites to test the hypotheses. Both marketing methods and data mining methods are utilized in the empirical testing.

## 3.2 THE MODEL

In this section, we describe the theoretical models that were developed. In the model, we consider five different shipping schedules. We formulate the cost that a rational shopper incurs under each shipping schedule, and derive the optimal purchase quantity for the shopper. By comparing the cost associated with each shipping schedule, we are able to draw conclusions about which shipping schedule a shopper will prefer. Furthermore, we investigate the relationship between price and the free shipping threshold (the total amount a shopper needs to spend in a purchase transaction in order to get free shipping). Our solution suggests that stores with different prices can be equally competitive if they offer free shipping at the right threshold.

### 3.2.1 Purchase Quantity and Cost for Different Shipping Schedules

Consider a risk-neutral shopper who purchases a product at an e-commerce Web site. Prior to the visit to the web site, the shopper chooses a purchasing level $Q$ on the basis of the prevailing price $p$. When the visitor arrives at the web site on his/her $n$th visit, however, the actual quantity purchased is $Q_n = Q + \varepsilon_n$, where $\varepsilon_n$ is a random element that captures the effect of non-price variables (e.g., other marketing mix variables such as special promotions or feature). The random shocks $\varepsilon_n$, $n \geq 1$ are i.i.d. with mean zero and variance $\sigma^2$. Let $\Phi$ denote the cumulative distribution function associated with $\varepsilon_n$.

Given the constant price, we assume a constant purchasing level $Q$ at every visit (i.e., on average, across all visits, the expected quantity purchased at every visit is $Q$). The shopper has a known constant consumption rate ($r$). We assume that the shopper will always have something to consume (i.e., whenever the shopper finishes the products bought in the last shopping trip, he/she will immediately buy more products). Suppose the shopper purchases $Q_n$ at the $n$th visit, then the elapsed time until the next purchase is given by $Q_n/r$. Under each shipping policy, the objective of the shopper is to choose the expected purchase quantity $Q$ so that the total long-run average relevant cost per unit time is minimized. The relevant cost includes the purchasing-related transaction cost $k$ (fixed), the inventory cost (or other costs associated with over-purchasing), the cost of purchase $pQ_n$ and shipping cost $S_n$. Inventory cost is charged at $h$ per unit time. The inventory cost incurred until the next purchase is given by $h \cdot Q_n/2 \cdot Q_n/r \cdot S_n$ and varies according to the shipping policy and the purchasing cost. If free shipping is available for every purchase transaction, $S_n$ is zero. If free shipping is never available, $S_n$ will depend on the actual shipping fee charged. We consider two types of shipping fee structures: one is a flat fee, and the other one is a variable fee (we use a linear fee structure). If free shipping is only available under certain conditions, $S_n$ will either be zero or the shipping fee charged. If the purchasing cost (or total dollar amount spent) exceeds the free shipping threshold $T$, $S_n$ is zero; if the purchasing cost does not exceed the free shipping threshold, $S_n$ is positive and its value depends on the shipping fee structure. This is further described below in the analysis.

The cost incurred by the shopper during the $n$th purchasing cycle is:

$$
C_n = \begin{cases} C_{n,l} = k + pQ_n + \dfrac{h}{2r}Q_n^2, & \text{if } pQ_n \geq T \\[2ex] C_{n,h} = k + S_n + pQ_n + \dfrac{h}{2r}Q_n^2, & \text{if } pQ_n < T \end{cases}
$$

We substitute $Q_n$ in the condition part with $Q_n = Q + \varepsilon_n$, then we get

$$
C_n =
\begin{cases}
C_{n,l} = k + pQ_n + \dfrac{h}{2r}Q_n^2, & \text{if } \varepsilon_n \geq \dfrac{T}{p} - Q \\[2ex]
C_{n,h} = k + S_n + pQ_n + \dfrac{h}{2r}Q_n^2, & \text{if } \varepsilon_n < \dfrac{T}{p} - Q
\end{cases}
$$

$S_n$ varies across different shipping fee schedules. We consider the following schedules:

S1: $T = 0$ (no shipping fee)

S2: $T \to \infty$ (no free shipping)

    S2.1: Fixed shipping fee: $S_n = K$

        $K$ is the flat fee charged.

    S2.2: Linear shipping fee: $S_n = cQ_n$, $(c > 0)$

        $c$ is the shipping charge for a unit of product.

S3: $T > 0$, but finite. (free shipping with a threshold)

    S3.1: Fixed shipping fee (if the free shipping threshold is not satisfied):

        $S_n = K$

    S3.2: Linear shipping fee (if the free shipping threshold is not satisfied):

        $S_n = cQ_n$, $(c > 0)$

Let $T_n$, $n \geq 1$ be the random variable that corresponds to the elapsed time until the next planned purchase after the $n$th visit:

$$
T_n = \frac{Q_n}{r} = \frac{Q + \varepsilon_n}{r}
$$

Because $\varepsilon_n$, $n \geq 1$ is i.i.d, the time until the next purchase, $T_n$, $n \geq 1$, is i.i.d. If $N(t)$ is the counting process that specifies the number of visits from time 0 to time $t$, $\{N(t), t \geq 0\}$ is a renewal process, and the time until the next planned purchase is a renewal cycle.

The total cost incurred at time $t$ is:

$$TC(t) = \sum_{n=1}^{N(t)} C_n$$

The expected total cost up to time $t$ is

$$E(TC(t)) = \sum_{n=1}^{N(t)} E(C_n) = \left(1 - \Phi\left(\frac{T}{p} - Q\right)\right) \sum_{n=1}^{N(t)} E(C_{n,l})$$

$$+ \Phi\left(\frac{T}{p} - Q\right) \sum_{n=1}^{N(t)} E(C_{n,h})$$

A shopper will choose the purchasing level $Q$ that will minimize the long run average cost per unit of time (LRACPUT):

$$\text{LRACPUT} = \underset{t \to \infty}{\text{Limit}} \frac{E(TC(t))}{t}$$

The result from Ross (1980) states that the long run average cost per unit of time is equal to the expected cost incurred during a renewal cycle ($\mu_C = E(C_n)$) divided by the expected length of the renewal cycle ($\mu_T = E(T_n)$).

$$\text{LRACPUT} = \frac{\mu_C}{\mu_T}$$

where:

$$\mu_T = \frac{Q}{r},$$

and

$$\mu_C = \left(1 - \Phi\left(\frac{T}{p} - Q\right)\right) E(C_{n,l}) + \Phi\left(\frac{T}{p} - Q\right) E(C_{n,h})$$

Now, $E(C_{n,l}) = k + pE(Q_n) + \dfrac{h}{2r} E(Q_n^2)$ and

$$E(Q_n^2) = Var(Q_n) + E(Q_n)^2 = \sigma^2 + Q^2,$$

hence:

$$\mu_C = \left(1-\Phi\left(\frac{T}{p}-Q\right)\right)\left(k+pQ+\frac{h}{2r}(Q^2+\sigma^2)\right)+\Phi\left(\frac{T}{p}-Q\right)E(C_{n,h})$$

Below, we determine $E(C_{n,h})$ under various shipping fee structures.

We assume that the distribution of the random shocks is uniform on an interval $[\alpha, \beta]$. Because the mean of the distribution is zero, it becomes a uniform distribution on $[-\beta, \beta]$, $(\beta > 0)$. And we have

$$\Phi\left(\frac{T}{p}-Q\right)=\frac{\left(\frac{T}{p}-Q\right)+\beta}{2\beta} \quad \text{and} \quad 1-\Phi\left(\frac{T}{p}-Q\right)=\frac{\beta-\left(\frac{T}{p}-Q\right)}{2\beta},$$

when $\dfrac{T}{p}-Q\in\left[-\beta,\beta\right]$

$$\Phi\left(\frac{T}{p}-Q\right)=0 \quad \text{and} \quad 1-\Phi\left(\frac{T}{p}-Q\right)=1, \quad \text{when} \quad \frac{T}{p}-Q<-\beta$$

$$\Phi\left(\frac{T}{p}-Q\right)=1 \quad \text{and} \quad 1-\Phi\left(\frac{T}{p}-Q\right)=0, \quad \text{when} \quad \frac{T}{p}-Q>\beta$$

**Scenario S1: $T=0$, (no shipping fee)**

$$E(C_{n,h})=k+pQ+\frac{h}{2r}(Q^2+\sigma^2)$$

$$\mu_C = \left(1-\Phi\left(\frac{T}{p}-Q\right)\right)\left(k+pQ+\frac{h}{2r}(Q^2+\sigma^2)\right)$$
$$+\Phi\left(\frac{T}{p}-Q\right)\left(k+pQ+\frac{h}{2r}(Q^2+\sigma^2)\right)$$

$$\mu_C = k + pQ + \frac{h}{2r}(Q^2 + \sigma^2)$$

$$\text{LRACPUT}(Q) = \frac{\mu_C}{\mu_T} = \frac{k + pQ + \dfrac{h}{2r}(Q^2 + \sigma^2)}{\dfrac{Q}{r}} \tag{1}$$

The function LRACPUT($Q$) takes on the form of a quadratic function divided by a linear function. In this case, we can apply Avriel's (1976, p.156) result that a function is pseudo convex when the function takes on the form of dividing a quadratic function by a linear function, to show that the function is pseudo-convex. We can then apply Theorem 6.7 in Avriel (1976), which states that the minimum of any pseudo-convex function satisfies the first order conditions, to show that the optimal purchasing policy ($Q^*$) must satisfy the first-order conditions (i.e. $\partial \text{LRACPUT}(Q)/\partial Q$). By taking the derivative of LRACPUT($Q$) in (1) with respect to $Q$ and by setting $\partial \text{LRACPUT}(Q)/\partial Q) = 0$, it is easy to show that the optimal purchasing policy is:

$$Q_{S1}^* = \sqrt{\frac{2kr}{h} + \sigma^2}$$

It is easy to see that $Q_{S1}^*$ will increase $\sigma^2$ as increases.

$$\text{LRACPUT}(Q_{S1}^*) = \sqrt{2krh + h^2\sigma^2} + rp$$

If we let $\hat{K}_{S1} = k + \dfrac{h}{2r}\sigma^2$, we can rewrite $Q_{S1}^*$ as

$$Q_{S1}^* = \sqrt{\frac{2r\hat{K}_{S1}}{h}}$$

When we plug $\hat{K}_{S1}$ and $Q_{S1}^*$ into LRACPUT($Q$), we get the optimal long run average cost per unit time:

$$\text{LRACPUT}(Q_{S1}^*) = \sqrt{2hr\hat{K}_{S1}} + rp$$

**Scenario S2.1: $T \to \infty$ (no free shipping) and flat shipping fee: $S_n = K$**

$$\mu_C = k + K + pQ + \frac{h}{2r}(Q^2 + \sigma^2)$$

$$\text{LRACPUT}(Q) = \frac{\mu_C}{\mu_T} = \frac{k + K + pQ + \dfrac{h}{2r}(Q^2 + \sigma^2)}{\dfrac{Q}{r}}$$

By setting $\partial\text{LRACPUT}(Q)/\partial Q = 0$, it is easy to show that the optimal purchasing policy is:

$$Q_{S2.1}^* = \sqrt{\frac{2(k+K)r}{h} + \sigma^2}$$

It is easy to see that $Q_{S2.2}^*$ will increase $\sigma^2$ as increases.

$$\text{LRACPUT}(Q_{S2.1}^*) = \sqrt{2(k+K)rh + h^2\sigma^2} + rp$$

If we let $\hat{K}_{S2.1} = k + K + \frac{h}{2r}\sigma^2$, we can rewrite $Q_{S2.1}^*$ as

$$Q_{S2.1}^* = \sqrt{\frac{2r\hat{K}_{S2.1}}{h}}$$

When we plug $\hat{K}_{S2.1}$ and $Q_{S2.1}^*$ into LRACPUT($Q$), we get the optimal long run average cost per unit time:

$$\text{LRACPUT}(Q_{S2.1}^*) = \sqrt{2hr\hat{K}_{S2.1}} + rp$$

**Scenario S2.2: $T \rightarrow \infty$ (no free shipping), and linear shipping fee: $S_n = cQ_n$, $(c > 0)$**

$$\mu_C = k + cQ + pQ + \frac{h}{2r}(Q^2 + \sigma^2)$$

$$\text{LRACPUT}(Q) = \frac{\mu_C}{\mu_T} = \frac{k + cQ + pQ + \frac{h}{2r}(Q^2 + \sigma^2)}{\frac{Q}{r}}$$

By setting $\partial \text{LRACPUT}(Q)/\partial Q = 0$, it is easy to show that the optimal purchasing policy is:

$$Q_{S2.2}^* = \sqrt{\frac{2kr}{h} + \sigma^2}$$

It is easy to see that $Q_{S2.2}^*$ will increase as $\sigma^2$ increases.

$$\text{LRACPUT}(Q_{S2.2}^*) = \sqrt{2krh + h^2\sigma^2} + r(c + p)$$

If we let $\hat{K}_{S2.2} = k + \frac{h}{2r}\sigma^2$, we can rewrite $Q_{S2.2}^*$ as

$$Q_{S2.2}^* = \sqrt{\frac{2r\hat{K}_{S2.2}}{h}}$$

When we plug $\hat{K}_{S2.2}$ and $Q_{S2.2}^*$ into LRACPUT($Q$), we get the optimal long run average cost per unit time:

$$\text{LRACPUT}(Q_{S2.2}^*) = \sqrt{2hr\hat{K}_{S2.2}} + r(c + p)$$

**Scenario S3.1: $T > 0$, but finite. (free shipping with a threshold), and flat shipping fee (if the free shipping threshold is not satisfied): $S_n = K$**

$$E(C_{n,h}) = k + K + pQ + \frac{h}{2r}(Q^2 + \sigma^2)$$

$$\mu_C = \left(1 - \Phi\left(\frac{T}{p} - Q\right)\right)\left(k + pQ + \frac{h}{2r}(Q^2 + \sigma^2)\right)$$
$$+ \Phi\left(\frac{T}{p} - Q\right)\left(k + K + pQ + \frac{h}{2r}(Q^2 + \sigma^2)\right)$$

When $\frac{T}{p} - Q \in [-\beta, \beta]$, that is $Q \in \left[\frac{T}{p} - \beta, \frac{T}{p} + \beta\right]$

$$\mu_C = \frac{\beta - \left(\frac{T}{p} - Q\right)}{2\beta}\left(k + pQ + \frac{h}{2r}(Q^2 + \sigma^2)\right)$$
$$+ \frac{\left(\frac{T}{p} - Q\right) + \beta}{2\beta}\left(k + K + pQ + \frac{h}{2r}(Q^2 + \sigma^2)\right)$$

$$\mu_C = \left(k + pQ + \frac{h}{2r}(Q^2 + \sigma^2)\right) + K\frac{\left(\frac{T}{p} - Q\right) + \beta}{2\beta}$$

$$\text{LRACPUT}(Q) = \frac{\mu_C}{\mu_T} = \frac{\left(k + pQ + \frac{h}{2r}(Q^2 + \sigma^2)\right) + K\frac{\left(\frac{T}{p} - Q\right) + \beta}{2\beta}}{\frac{Q}{r}}$$

By setting $\partial\text{LRACPUT}(Q)/\partial Q = 0$, it is easy to show that the optimal purchasing policy is:

$$Q^*_{S3.1} = \sqrt{\frac{2kr}{h} + \sigma^2 + \frac{rK\left(\frac{T}{p} + \beta\right)}{\beta h}}$$

It is easy to see that $Q^*_{S3.1}$ will increase with $T$ and $\sigma^2$.

$$\text{LRACPUT}(Q^*_{S3.1}) = \sqrt{2krh + h^2\sigma^2 + \frac{KrhT}{p\beta} + Krh + rp} \qquad (2)$$

If we let $\hat{K}_{S3.1} = k + \frac{h}{2r}\sigma^2 + \frac{K}{2\beta}\left(\frac{T}{p} + \beta\right)$, we can rewrite $Q^*_{S3.1}$ as

$$Q^*_{S3.1} = \sqrt{\frac{2r\hat{K}_{S3.1}}{h}}$$

When we plug $\hat{K}_{S3.1}$ and $Q^*_{S3.1}$ into LRACPUT(Q), we get the optimal long run average cost per unit time:

$$\text{LRACPUT}(Q^*_{S3.1}) = \sqrt{2hr\hat{K}_{S3.1}} + rp$$

When $T/P - Q < \beta$, that is $Q > T/P + \beta$:

$$\mu_C = k + pQ + \frac{h}{2r}(Q^2 + \sigma^2)$$

$$Q^*_{S3.1} = \sqrt{\frac{2kr}{h} + \sigma^2}$$

$$\text{LRACPUT}(Q^*_{S3.1}) = \sqrt{2hr\hat{K}_{S3.1a}} + rp, \quad \text{where } \hat{K}_{S3.1a} = k + \frac{h}{2r}\sigma^2$$

The solutions ($Q^*$ and LRACPUT($Q^*$)) are exactly the same as the solutions in S1 (no shipping fee). The implication is that when the threshold $T$ and the quantity variation $\beta$ are small enough, the quantity purchased will be high enough that the shoppers can always get free shipping, which is exactly the same as the situation in S1.

When $T/P - Q > \beta$, that is $Q < T/P - \beta$:

$$\mu_C = k + K + pQ + \frac{h}{2r}(Q^2 + \sigma^2)$$

$$Q_{S3.1}^* = \sqrt{\frac{2(k+K)r}{h} + \sigma^2}$$

$$\text{LRACPUT}(Q_{S3.1}^*) = \sqrt{2hr\hat{K}_{S3.1b}} + rp, \text{ where } \hat{K}_{S3.1b} = k + K + \frac{h}{2r}\sigma^2$$

The solutions ($Q^*$ and LRACPUT($Q^*$)) are exactly the same as the solutions in S2.1 (no free shipping, flat fee). Under extreme situations, S3.1 will either degenerate to S1 or S2.1. In the comparison we draw later, we do not discuss these two extreme cases.

**Scenario S3.2: $T>0$, but finite. (free shipping with a threshold), and linear shipping fee (if the free shipping threshold is not satisfied): $S_n = cQ_n$, $(c>0)$**

$$E(C_{n,h}) = k + (p+c)Q + \frac{h}{2r}(Q^2 + \sigma^2)$$

$$\mu_C = \left(1 - \Phi\left(\frac{T}{p} - Q\right)\right)\left(k + pQ + \frac{h}{2r}(Q^2 + \sigma^2)\right)$$

$$+ \Phi\left(\frac{T}{p} - Q\right)\left(k + (p+c)Q + \frac{h}{2r}(Q^2 + \sigma^2)\right)$$

When $\frac{T}{p} - Q \in [-\beta, \beta]$, that is $Q \in \left[\frac{T}{p} - \beta, \frac{T}{p} + \beta\right]$

$$\mu_C = \frac{\beta - \left(\frac{T}{p} - Q\right)}{2\beta}\left(k + pQ + \frac{h}{2r}(Q^2 + \sigma^2)\right)$$

$$+ \frac{\left(\frac{T}{p} - Q\right) + \beta}{2\beta}\left(k + (p+c)Q + \frac{h}{2r}(Q^2 + \sigma^2)\right)$$

$$\mu_C = \left(k + pQ + \frac{h}{2r}(Q^2 + \sigma^2)\right) + c\frac{\left(\frac{T}{p} - Q\right) + \beta}{2\beta}Q$$

$$\text{LRACPUT}(Q) = \frac{\mu_C}{\mu_T} = \frac{\left(k + pQ + \frac{h}{2r}(Q^2 + \sigma^2)\right) + c\dfrac{\left(\frac{T}{p} - Q\right) + \beta}{2\beta}Q}{\dfrac{Q}{r}}$$

By setting $\partial \text{LRACPUT}(Q)/\partial Q = 0$, it is easy to show that the optimal purchasing policy is:

$$Q_{S3.2}^* = \sqrt{\frac{k + \dfrac{h}{2r}\sigma^2}{\dfrac{h}{2r} - \dfrac{c}{2\beta}}}$$

It's easy to see that $Q_{S3.2}^*$ will increase with $T$ and $\sigma^2$. We also observe that

$$Q_{S3.2}^* = \sqrt{\frac{k + \dfrac{h}{2r}\sigma^2}{\dfrac{h}{2r} - \dfrac{c}{2\beta}}} > \sqrt{\frac{k + \dfrac{h}{2r}\sigma^2}{\dfrac{h}{2r}}} = \sqrt{\frac{2kr}{h} + \sigma^2}$$

If we plug $Q_{S3.2}^*$ into LRACPUT($Q$), we get the optimal long run average cost per unit time:

$$\text{LRACPUT}(Q_{S3.2}^*) = 2r\sqrt{\left(k + \frac{h}{2r}\sigma^2\right)\left(\frac{h}{2r} - \frac{c}{2\beta}\right)} + rp$$

$$+ \frac{rc}{2\beta}\left(\frac{T}{p} + \beta\right)$$

(3)

$$\frac{T}{p} - Q < -\beta$$

Also following the same discussion in S3.1, we have two extreme situations under S3.2. When $\frac{T}{p} - Q < -\beta$ , S3.2 will degenerate to S1. And when $\frac{T}{p} - Q > \beta$ , S3.2 will degenerate to S2.2. Again, we do not include these two extreme cases in later comparisons.

### 3.2.2 Relationship between Shipping Threshold (T) and Price (p)

**Scenario S3.1: T>0, but finite. (free shipping with a threshold), and flat shipping fee (if the free shipping threshold is not satisfied): $S_n = K$**

From equation (2)

$$\text{LRACPUT}(Q^*_{S3.1}) = \sqrt{2krh + h^2\sigma^2 + \frac{KrhT}{p\beta} + Krh + rp}, \text{ we can set}$$

$\text{LRACPUT}(Q^*_{S3.1})$ be a constant $C$, and solve for the relationship between $T$ and $p$.

$$T = \frac{p\beta(C^2 - 2krh - Krh - 2rpC + p^2r^2 - h^2\sigma^2)}{Krh} \tag{4}$$

This is a cubic function of $p$ that has 3 roots. We solve for these roots and get:

$$\left\{ r_1 = 0, r_2 = \frac{C - \sqrt{2krh + Krh + h^2\sigma^2}}{r}, r_3 = \frac{C + \sqrt{2krh + Krh + h^2\sigma^2}}{r} \right\}$$

Because

$$\text{LRACPUT}(Q^*_{S3.1}) = \sqrt{2krh + h^2\sigma^2 + \frac{KrhT}{p\beta} + Krh + rp}$$

$$> \sqrt{2krh + Krh + h^2\sigma^2},$$

we have $\dfrac{C - \sqrt{2krh + Krh + h^2\sigma^2}}{r} > 0$. The second and third roots of the cubic function will always be positive, and the cubic function will look like the following.

FIGURE 15.    Cubic Function (4)

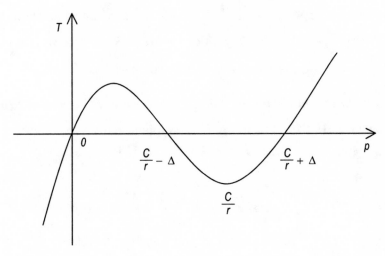

From equation (2), we can see that LRACPUT ($Q^*_{S3.1}$) > $rp$, which means that the feasible region for $p$ in Figure 15 is $P < C/r$ After considering the feasible values for $T$ ($T$ needs to be no less than 0, we also consider only positive $p > 0$), we have the following relationship between feasible $T$ and $p$.

FIGURE 16.    Feasible $T$ and $p$

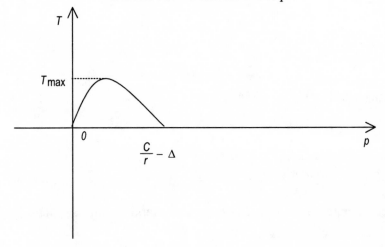

$T_{max}$ can be reached at the local maximum. By taking the first order condition of $T$ in respect to $p$ in equation (4) ( by setting $\dfrac{\partial T}{\partial p} = 0$ ), we get the two local max/min:

$$p = \frac{2Ch}{3r^2} \pm \frac{1}{3r}\sqrt{C^2 + 6krh + 3Krh + 3h^2\sigma^2}$$

From Figure 15, it is easy to see that $T_{max}$ is reached at the smaller $p$,

$$p_{max} = \frac{2Ch}{3r^2} - \frac{1}{3r}\sqrt{C^2 + 6krh + 3Krh + 3h^2\sigma^2}$$

$T$ will increase with $p$ at first and then decrease as $p$ increases.

**Scenario S3.2: $T>0$, but finite. (free shipping with a threshold), and linear shipping fee (if the free shipping threshold is not satisfied): $S_n = cQ_n$, $(c>0)$**

Following the same analysis above, we get the following relationship between T and p from equation (3).

$$T = -\frac{rc}{2\beta}p\left[2r\sqrt{\left(k+\frac{h}{2r}\sigma^2\right)\left(\frac{h}{2r}-\frac{c}{2\beta}\right)}+\frac{rc}{2}-C+rp\right] \tag{5}$$

The two roots are:

$$\left\{0, \frac{C}{r}-2\sqrt{\left(k+\frac{h}{2r}\sigma^2\right)\left(\frac{h}{2r}-\frac{c}{2\beta}\right)}-\frac{c}{2}\right\}$$

Because

$$\mathrm{LRACPUT}(Q^*_{S3.2}) = 2r\sqrt{\left(k+\frac{h}{2r}\sigma^2\right)\left(\frac{h}{2r}-\frac{c}{2\beta}\right)}+rp+\frac{rc}{2\beta}\left(\frac{T}{p}+\beta\right)$$

$$> 2r\sqrt{\left(k+\frac{h}{2r}\sigma^2\right)\left(\frac{h}{2r}-\frac{c}{2\beta}\right)}+rp+\frac{rc}{2},$$

we have $C > 2r\sqrt{\left(k + \dfrac{h}{2r}\sigma^2\right)\left(\dfrac{h}{2r} - \dfrac{c}{2\beta}\right)} + \dfrac{rc}{2}$, which means that the second root is positive. It's also clear that $T > 0$, so we have the following figure describing the relationship between $T$ and $p$.

FIGURE 17.   Feasible $T$ and $p$ in Function (5)

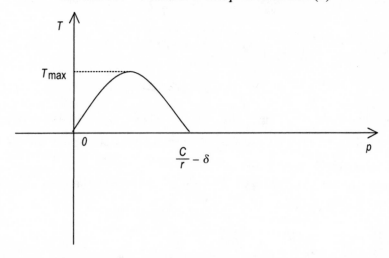

By taking the first order condition of $T$ in respect to $p$ in equation (5) ( by setting $\dfrac{\partial T}{\partial p} = 0$ ), we get the local maximum:

$$p_{max} = \frac{C}{2r} - \sqrt{\left(k + \frac{h}{2r}\sigma^2\right)\left(\frac{h}{2r} - \frac{c}{2\beta}\right)} - \frac{c}{4}$$

Under both cases, $T$ and $p$ follow a similar relationship, $T$ will first increase with $p$ and then decrease with $p$. The line in Figure 16 or Figure 17 is the line with fixed LRACPUT. It indicates that every point in that line will have the same cost for shoppers. It further implies that stores with different price levels can be equally competitive by choosing the right free shipping threshold $T$.

### 3.2.3 Comparisons

We can see that:

$$Q_{S1}^{*}* = Q_{S2.2}^{*}, \ Q_{S2.1}^{*} > Q_{S1}^{*}, \ Q_{S3.1}^{*} > Q_{S1}^{*}, \ Q_{S3.2}^{*} > Q_{S1}^{*}$$

If $T > \beta p$, we'll have $Q_{S3.1}^{*} > Q_{S2.1}^{*}$.

It's clear that $\hat{K}_{S2.1} > \hat{K}_{S1}, \hat{K}_{S3.1} > \hat{K}_{S1}$, so

$$\text{LRACPUT}(Q_{S2.1}^{*}) > \text{LRACPUT}(Q_{S1}^{*})$$

$$\text{LRACPUT}(Q_{S3.1}^{*}) > \text{LRACPUT}(Q_{S1}^{*})$$

Because $c + p > p$ and $\hat{K}_{S2.2} > \hat{K}_{S1}$, we have

$$\text{LRACPUT}(Q_{S2.2}^{*}) > \text{LRACPUT}(Q_{S1}^{*})$$

If $T > \beta p$, we'll have $\hat{K}_{S3.1} > \hat{K}_{S2.1}$ which implies that

$$\text{LRACPUT}(Q_{S3.1}^{*}) > \text{LRACPUT}(Q_{2.1}^{*})$$

This indicates that shoppers will prefer a no-free-shipping flat free policy to a free shipping policy (under flat fee charges if not qualified) with a high enough threshold.

Under some situations, it can be true that $\text{LRACPUT}(Q_{S3.2}^{*}) > \text{LRACPUT}(Q_{S1}^{*})$, which means that shoppers do not necessarily prefer S1 (no shipping fee) to S3.2 (free shipping with threshold, linear fee).

**Proposition 1.** *The average purchase quality is irrelevant to the threshold under a linear fee shipping policy.*

**Proposition 2.** *A rational shopper will buy the same average quantity at a visit under both S1 (no shipping fee) and S2.2 (no free shipping, linear fee), and will buy more under S2.1 (no free shipping, flat fee), S3.1 (free shipping with threshold, flat fee) and S3.2 (free shipping with threshold, linear fee). If $T > \beta p$, the shopper will buy more under S3.1 than S2.1.*

**Proposition 3.**   *A rational shopper will prefer S1 (no shipping fee) to S2.1, S2.2, and S3.1, but not necessarily S3.2. If the threshold is high enough, the shopper will prefer S2.1 (no free shipping, flat fee) to S3.1 (flat fee, free shipping with threshold).*

### 3.2.4 Hypotheses

> *HYPOTHESIS 1. The average purchase quantity is higher for a store with higher purchase variability than for a store with lower purchase variability. (This applies for all shipping fee policies).*

> *HYPOTHESIS 2. If a store has a higher threshold for free shipping, the average purchase quantity is also higher under a flat fee (non-linear with decreasing average shipping cost per product) shipping policy.*

> *HYPOTHESIS 3. We will observe wider price dispersion when the free shipping threshold is lower.*

## 3.3 EMPIRICAL ANALYSIS AND HYPOTHESIS TESTING

### 3.3.1 Data Description

We use the comScore panelist-level (a panelist is a selected household) web behavior database which captures detailed browsing and buying behavior of 100,000 Internet users between July 2002 and Dec. 2002. The panel is based on a random sample from a cross-section of more than 1.5 million global Internet users who have given comScore explicit permission to confidentially capture their Web-wide activity. The data includes information regarding which sites individuals purchase from, when they purchase, what they purchase, and how much they pay. The demographics of these panelists are also provided in the database.

## 3.3.2 Hypothesis Testing: Average Quantity and Quantity Variance

We test Hypothesis 1 by comparing the relative quantity and quantity variability across different pairs of Web sites. We picked different pairs of Web sites selling books and CDs (assuming that each Web site is selling one single product – books or CDs). The average and variance of purchase quantity are calculated among all purchase transactions on a Web site containing just books or just CDs. The quantity of a purchase transaction is the total number of books/CDs bought in the transaction (not the number of books/CDs with the same title). This assumption is useful when analyzing Web data, since, unlike traditional stores, shoppers seldom buy exactly the same product more than once in a single purchase transaction. Books and CDs have the property of sharing similar prices within the category. In Tables 10 and 11, we present the results on 5 CD Web sites, and 3 book Web sites. It shows that as quantity variance gets lower, the average quantity also gets lower.

We also conducted analysis within a Web site. For a Web site, we grouped customers into two groups: one with higher purchase quantity variance, one with lower purchase quantity variance. We checked whether the higher variance group also had higher average purchase quantity. When we checked the difference between the average purchase quantity, we also measured whether average purchase price differed between the two groups. In addition, we also used a data mining tool called *contrast set* to check whether there were any other significant differences between the demographics of the two groups. The demographics include education level, census region, household size, household oldest age, household income, child present or not, racial background, connection speed, and

TABLE 10.   Average Q and Q Variance at 5 Web sites Selling CDs

|  | columbiahouse | cduniverse | towerrecords | cdnow | Samgoody |
|---|---|---|---|---|---|
| Variance | 10.306593 | 7.38381 | 5.03958 | 2.170561 | 0.9439024 |
| Q-mean | 4.521352 | 2.573034 | 2.318519 | 1.857831 | 1.6097561 |

TABLE 11. Average Q and Q variance at 3 Web sites Selling Books

|  | christianbook | bn | booksamillion |
|---|---|---|---|
| Variance | 34.719576 | 5.367325 | 4.025254 |
| Q-mean | 4.317422 | 2.576162 | 2.414966 |

TABLE 12. Comparisons Between Two Groups on Different Web sites

|  | bn.com | cdnow.com | columbiahouse.com | cduniverse.com |
|---|---|---|---|---|
| Average purchase quantity | Significant different ($p<0.001$) | Significant different ($p=0.0026$) | Significant different ($p=0.016$) | Significant different ($p=0.0487$) |
| Average purchase price | Significant different ($p=0.089$) | No significant different ($p=0.8697$) | Significant different ($p<0.001$) | Significant different ($p=0.0529$) |
| Demographic profiles | No significant difference | No significant difference | No significant difference | No significant difference |

country of origin. Contrast set methods proposed by Bay and Pazzani (2001) can detect whether there are (statistically) significant differences between two groups. They not only consider the difference for a single attribute, but also consider the difference for a combination of attributes (see Appendix 3 for detailed descriptions). Among the 8 Web sites we list in Table 10 and 11, there are four Web sites with enough data for us to conduct this analysis, and the results are shown in Table 12.

It is apparent that for all four Web sites, there are differences between the average purchase quantities of the two groups; some are caused by the difference in price, and some are not. The demographics of these groups are not significantly different.

### 3.3.3 Hypothesis Testing: Threshold Level and Purchase Quantity

To test this hypothesis, we measured how quantity changed under different thresholds on the same Web site. For the period of time when the data is available, Amazon.com had changed its threshold level. From

July 1, 2003 to Aug. 24, 2003, customers were eligible for free shipping if the order amount exceeded $49; from Aug. 25, 2003 to Oct. 18, 2002, that threshold was $25. We set the length of the two periods to be equal by excluding the holiday period (Oct. 19 – Dec. 31). In the $49 period, the average purchase quantity was 3.31, and in the $25 period, the average purchase quantity was 2.53. The results match hypothesis 2.

### 3.3.4 Hypothesis Testing: Threshold and Price Dispersion

This hypothesis is tested using data from amazon.com. We picked all the books and CDs that are purchased more than once in both the time period with the $49 threshold (July 1 – Aug. 24) and the time period with the $25 threshold (Aug. 25 – Oct. 18). For each product, we calculated the price dispersion (the difference between the maximum price and the minimum price) in each period. We used the following regression model to test the relationship between the threshold and the price dispersion.

$$Price\_dispersion = \alpha + \beta T$$

T is 0 for the $49 period and 1 for the $25 period. The result is as follows.

```
Coefficients:
              Value Std. Error  t value  Pr(>|t|)
(Intercept)  6.5723 2.5094       2.6191   0.0116
        T    4.0623 2.5094       1.6188   0.1118

Residual standard error: 18.1 on 50 degrees of freedom
Multiple R-Squared: 0.0498
F-statistic: 2.621 on 1 and 50 degrees of freedom,
the p-value is 0.1118
```

We can see that $\beta$ is positive indicating that the price dispersion is higher in the $25 period. The average price dispersion in the $49 period is $2.51. For the $25 period the average price dispersion is $10.63.

## 3.4 LITERATURE REVIEW

As mentioned in the introduction, we have not been able to identify similar research that addresses free shipping related issues. However, there are few papers that touch on this issue. Morwitz et al. (1998) conducted behavioral experiments to test the effect of partitioned price. In one of the experiments they conducted, they presented subjects with different price formats: (1) combined price: "$82.90, including shipping and handling;" (2) base price and surcharge in dollars: "$69.95 plus $12.95 for shipping and handling;" and (3) base price and surcharge in percentage terms: "$69.95 plus 18.5% for shipping and handling." All the three formats create the same total product cost. Their results suggest that partitioned prices decrease total costs recalled by consumers and increase demand. The behavioral findings in Morwitz et al. (1998) give us further support for the importance of the free-shipping issue we study in this essay.

Hess et al. (1996) observed that catalog marketers use a pricing scheme in which they charge a separate shipping and handling fee which is not refundable when a product is returned. Many direct marketers offer price refunds to unsatisfied consumers, but as a result some consumers order products with no intention of keeping them. Hess et al. (1996) show that such returns can be controlled in a profitable way by imposing non-refundable charges such that these charges increase with the value of the merchandise ordered. Data collected from clothing mail-order catalogs is consistent with their theory. The shipping and handling charges of these catalogs are usually non-refundable and increase with the value of the merchandised ordered even when the actual shipping and handling costs are constant.

## 3.5 CONCLUSION: CONTRIBUTIONS, LIMITATIONS AND FUTURE WORK

In this essay, we analyze the impact of different free-shipping schedules on the shopping behavior of a rational shopper. The closed-form solutions enable us to elegantly characterize the optimal shopping policy of a rational shopper and to examine the difference among free-shipping schedules.

Our results show that two stores with different price levels can be equally competitive by choosing the right free-shipping threshold. We tested some hypotheses generated from the theoretical model using Internet purchasing data from various Web sites. Overall, the data support our predictions.

There are also limitations. In order for our analytical solution to be tractable, we unavoidably had to make certain assumptions. (1) We assume that the purchase quantity will be positive for each shopping trip. Given that we study Internet retailers, we need to investigate the effect of such an assumption in more detail. (2) We also assume that the shopper incurs inventory cost and we need to study more about the conditions when this is the case. (3) We assume a fixed consumption rate. This may be restricted to certain types of products (e.g. milk). We need to study the appropriateness of this assumption for the types of products people buy from the Internet (or we can extend the model to deal with a changing consumption rate). (4) We set up the model to minimize the shopper's cost, and in turn study the store's policy based on the rational behavior of the shoppers. In future work we will investigate setting this up as a profit maximizing model for the firms in a competitive setting. (5) We only have half a year of data. This poses some restrictions on the ability of controlling for seasonality. The empirical tests might be even more convincing if more data were available.

In the future, we plan to extend the research as follows: (1) We plan to build a store-level profit-maximizing model for two competitive stores. Given different pairs of shipping policies two different stores may have, we will study shopper behavior and suggest the best shipping policies for two competing stores based on the shoppers' reactions. (2) In this paper, we consider only rational shoppers. In the future, we plan to study shoppers with certain irrational behaviors, and see if our conclusions change.

# Part IV

# Conclusion

# 4

# CONCLUSION

Both data mining and marketing research study marketing problems such as market segmentation and promotion planning. While the two research communities share the same interests, their methodologies are quite different. This research studies two marketing problems (customer segmentation and promotion planning) using both data mining and marketing methods/models. In so doing, this research sheds light on the differences between these two research disciplines. For the customer segmentation problem addressed in the first essay, we develop new data mining methods and apply them to customer segmentation problems. Other two popular methods from the marketing literature are used in the evaluation step of the essay. We show how data mining methods can help solve customer segmentation problems in a data rich environment. The second essay focuses on a specific marketing problem: the relationship between free shipping promotions and Internet shopping behavior. In this essay we developed original analytical models that generated hypotheses

82

THE ONLINE CUSTOMER

that were tested on the Internet data. A data mining method called *contrast set* was also used for empirical testing. Each essay was evaluated independently on different data sets which originated from the Web.

In the first essay, we show how data mining concepts such as patterns can be used to help represent the underlying behavior governing the generation of the data and how the flexibility in representation can help us develop more effective methods in discovering segments in data and build more accurate predictive models. We study a new approach to segmenting customer transactions that is based on the idea that natural behavioral patterns may exist in different groups of transactions. At the highest level, the idea is to cluster customer transactions such that patterns generated from each cluster, while similar to each other within the cluster, are very different from the patterns generated from other clusters. Techniques are also developed to help achieve this goal. We further developed a modeling framework for building segment-level predictive models based on the pattern-based clustering approach and signature discovery techniques. We evaluated our pattern-based clustering and model-building approach using different experiments involving 90 different datasets generated from the Web. In each experiment, we compared our approach with several segmentation approaches in data mining and marketing and demonstrate that our approach is highly effective.

In the second essay, we analyze the impact of different free-shipping schedules on the shopping behavior of a rational shopper. We developed original analytical models and derived closed-form solutions that enabled us to elegantly characterize the optimal shopping policy of a rational shopper and examined the difference among various free-shipping schedules. Our model results show that two stores with different price levels can be equally competitive by choosing the right free-shipping threshold. We also tested some hypotheses generated from the theoretical model using Internet purchasing data from various Web sites. Overall, the results support our predictions. In our method, we used both common marketing approaches and a data mining method.

By studying two marketing problems using both data mining and marketing methodologies, we provide insights about the value of both research streams in addressing marketing problems.

## 4.1 CONTRIBUTIONS

***Essay 1. Pattern-based Clustering***   The main contribution of this essay is the development of this novel clustering approach that is based on the concept of pattern difference and similarity. We further use the proposed clustering approach to help build more accurate predictive models. Extensive experiments demonstrate the effectiveness of the approach.

***Essay 2. Free-shipping Promotions and Internet Shopping Behavior*** The main contribution of this essay is that we study an important Internet marketing problem that has not been studied much before. We analyzed the impact of different free-shipping schedules on the shopping behavior of a rational shopper and derived closed-form solutions for various questions we want to address. The analysis has enabled us to elegantly characterize the optimal shopping policy of a rational shopper and examine the difference among different free-shipping schedules. Our results also reveal the relationship between price and the free-shipping threshold and suggest that two retailers with different price levels can be equally competitive by choosing the right free-shipping threshold. We also empirically tested some hypotheses derived from the theoretical model using Internet purchase data from various Web sites. Overall, the results support our predictions.

## 4.2 LIMITATIONS AND FUTURE WORK

The broader objective of the research was to study how data mining and marketing approaches can be used to study marketing problems. In particular, we sought to integrate and compare methods from the marketing and data mining fields. The research used both approaches to address specific problems.

For the first essay, we observe the following limitations. (1) As the empirical work demonstrates, some segmentation approaches perform better for certain data sets than for others. We conducted extensive experiments to investigate the performance of different approaches, but we are unable to identify the factors affecting performance. Future research should investigate such factors. This may involve manipulating synthetic data sets, controlling different sets of parameters of the segmentation approaches, or conducting deeper computational analysis. (2) We provide a heuristic-based algorithm for pattern-based clustering and empirically demonstrate that the algorithm is effective, but we do not study how close to optimal the solution is. (3) The comparison conducted in this essay is among several chosen approaches. A wider selection – especially selecting an item/itemset/rule base – is desirable. (4) Using more types of data sets to further test the performance of various approaches should also provide more insights.

In addition to addressing the limitations, we also plan to extend this research along the following directions. (1) In this essay, we use itemsets to represent patterns, and developed the associated objective function and algorithm for the representation. As pointed out earlier, there exists the opportunity to extend the method to different pattern representations, such as rules and sequences. (2) There is also the potential to refine the objective function and algorithm for different applications (e.g. DNA sequence analysis, text clustering, stock clustering, etc.) since there is domain specific knowledge of different applications that can facilitate the development of more effective methods.

For essay two, we observe the following limitations. In order for our analytical solution to be tractable, we unavoidably had to make certain assumptions. (1) We assume that the purchase quantity will be positive for each shopping trip. Given that we study Internet retailers, we need to investigate the effect of such an assumption in more detail. (2) We also assume that the shoppers incur inventory cost and we need to study more about the conditions when this is the case. (3) We assume a fixed consumption rate. This may be restricted to certain type of products (e.g. milk). We need to study the appropriateness of this assumption for the types of products people buy from the Internet (or extend the model to deal with a changing consumption rate). (4) We set up the model to minimize the shopper's cost, and in turn study the store's policy based on the rational behavior of the shoppers. In future work we will investigate setting this up as a profit maximizing model for the firms in a competitive setting. (5) We only have half a year of data. This poses some restrictions on the ability to control for seasonality. Finally, empirical testing will be even more convincing when more data are available.

In the future, we plan to do the following extensions. (1) We plan to build a store-level profit-maximizing model for two competitive stores. Given different pairs of shipping policies two different stores may have, we will study shopper behavior and then suggest the best shipping policies for two competing stores based on the shoppers' reactions. (2) In this essay, we consider only rational shoppers. In the future, we plan to study shoppers with certain irrational behaviors, and see if our conclusions change.

# APPENDIX 1. PROOF

## MOTIVATION FOR DEFINITION 1 (DIFFERENCE BETWEEN TWO CLUSTERS)

Let $D$ be a set of transactions to be clustered. Let $I = \{i_1, i_2, \ldots, i_m\}$ be a set of literals, called items. Each transaction $T$ is a set of items such that $T \subseteq I$. We say that a transaction $T$ contains $B$, a set of some items in $I$, if $B \subseteq T$. Let $U$ be the set of all non-empty subsets of $I$. $U = \{B_1, B_2, \ldots, B_q\}$, where $q = 2^m - 1$. The probability of a transaction containing $B_k$ ($0 \leq k \leq q$) is $P(B_k \subseteq T)$.

Assuming that there are two latent states generating all transactions in a probabilistic manner, we will show that our difference definition is "good" because it is maximized when the clusters are pure. Under each state, assume that a set of probabilities is followed in generating transactions. Table 13 represents the two sets of probabilities. For each $B_k$ ($0 \leq k \leq q$), the probability for $B_k$ occurring in a transaction in state 1 ($S_a$) and in state 2 ($S_b$) are $P_k^a$ and $P_k^b$, respectively.

Assume that $D$ is divided into two clusters, $C_1$ and $C_2$. Within $C_1$, the percentage of transactions generated under $S_a$ is $P_x$ and the percentage of transactions generated under $S_b$ is $(1 - P_x)$. Within $C_2$, the percentage of transactions generated under $S_a$ is $P_y$ and the percentage of transactions generated under $S_b$ is $(1 - P_y)$. The distribution is further illustrated in Table 14.

TABLE 13.  Probabilities Under 2 States

| State 1 ($S_a$) | State 2 ($S_b$) |
|---|---|
| $P_1^a = P(B_1 \subseteq T \mid S_a)$ | $P_1^b = P(B_1 \subseteq T \mid S_b)$ |
| $P_2^a = P(B_2 \subseteq T \mid S_a)$ | $P_2^b = P(B_2 \subseteq T \mid S_b)$ |
| ... | ... |
| $P_q^b = P(B_q \subseteq T \mid S_a)$ | $P_q^b = P(B_q \subseteq T \mid S_b)$ |

TABLE 14.    Distribution of Transactions

|  | $C_1$ | $C_2$ |
|---|---|---|
| From $S_a$ | $P_x$ | $P_y$ |
| From $S_b$ | $1-P_x$ | $1-P_y$ |
|  | $0 \leq P_x, P_y \leq 1$ | |

In $C_1$, the expected percentage of transactions containing $B_k$ $(0 \leq k \leq q)$ is:

$$P_x \cdot P_k^a + (1 - P_x) \cdot P_k^b \quad \text{(denoted by SUPPORT}_{ak})$$

In $C_2$, the expected percentage of transactions containing $B_k (0 \leq k \leq q)$ is:

$$P_y \cdot P_k^a + (1 - P_y) \cdot P_k^b \quad \text{(denoted by SUPPORT}_{bk})$$

**Lemma 1.** $\sum_{k=1}^{q} \left| \text{SUPPORT}_{ak} - \text{SUPPORT}_{bk} \right|$ *is maximized when transactions generated from $S_a$ and $S_b$ are correctly separated (i.e. clusters are pure).*

*Proof:*

$$\left| \text{SUPPORT}_{ak} - \text{SUPPORT}_{bk} \right|$$

$$= \left| [P_x \cdot P_k^a + (1 - P_x) \cdot P_k^b] - [P_y \cdot P_k^a + (1 - P_y) \cdot P_k^b] \right|$$

$$= \left| (P_x - P_y) \cdot (P_k^a - P_k^b) \right|$$

$$= \left| P_x - P_y \right| \cdot \left| P_k^a - P_k^b \right| \tag{A1.1}$$

This difference is clearly maximized when $|P_x - P_y| = 1$, which is the case when the clusters are pure (i.e. either $(P_x = 1, P_y = 0)$ or $(P_x = 0, P_y = 1)$).

It naturally follows that $\sum_{k=1}^{q} (\text{SUPPORT}_{ak} - \text{SUPPORT}_{bk})$ is maximized when the clusters are pure.

We do not just consider a single itemset (one $B_k$) or a small subset of itemsets as the patterns distinguishing two clusters, even though (A1.1) (single itemset case) is also maximized when the clusters are pure. The reason is that $\left| P_k^a - P_k^b \right|$ may be zero for some $B_k$, and (A1.1) will be zero under this case. No matter how we cluster, the support difference between two clusters will always be zero. By choosing all of the frequent itemsets in the dataset, we can avoid this problem as well as the problem of considering too many itemsets ($q = 2^m - 1$).

Hence, if we define our difference function as (A1.2), the difference between two clusters will be maximized when the transactions are correctly clustered.

$$\text{Difference}(C_1, C_2) = \sum_{k=1}^{q} \left| \text{SUPPORT}_{ak} - \text{SUPPORT}_{bk} \right| \qquad \text{(A1.2)}$$

We have shown that the correct clustering of the set of transactions $D$ will be achieved by maximizing the difference between two clusters (A1.2) under the distributional assumption in Table 13. Definition (A1.2) is a simpler form of Definition 1 that was proposed in Section 2. We argue, in Section 2, that incorporating the relative difference into the definition of difference is more intuitive. Here we prove that Definition 1 shares the same property as Definition (A1.2) in that it will be maximized when the correct clustering is achieved.

**Proposition 1.** $\displaystyle\sum_{k=1}^{q} \frac{\left| \text{SUPPORT}_{ak} - \text{SUPPORT}_{bk} \right|}{\frac{1}{2}(\text{SUPPORT}_{ak} + \text{SUPPORT}_{bk})}$ *is maximized when transactions generated from* $S_a$ *and* $S_b$ *are correctly separated.*

*Proof:*

$$\text{SUPPORT}_{ak} + \text{SUPPORT}_{bk}$$
$$= \left[ P_x \cdot P_k^a + (1 - P_x) \cdot P_k^b \right] + \left[ P_y \cdot P_k^a + (1 - P_y) \cdot P_k^b \right]$$
$$= 2 \cdot P_k^b + (P_x + P_y) \cdot (P_k^a - P_k^b) \qquad \text{(A1.3)}$$

From both (A1.1) and (A1.3), we get

$$R = \frac{\left| SUPPORT_{ak} - SUPPORT_{bk} \right|}{SUPPORT_{ak} + SUPPORT_{bk}} = \frac{\left| (P_x - P_y) \cdot (P_k^a - P_k^b) \right|}{2 \cdot P_k^b + (P_x + P_y) \cdot (P_k^a - P_k^b)}$$

When the two clusters are pure, $R$ becomes

$$R^* = \frac{\left| 1 \cdot (P_k^a - P_k^b) \right|}{2 \cdot P_k^b + 1 \cdot (P_k^a - P_k^b)} = \frac{\left| P_k^a - P_k^b \right|}{P_k^a + P_k^b}$$

We first prove that there does not exist, $P_x$, $P_y$, $P_k^a$, $P_k^b$ ($0 < P_x$, $P_y$, $P_k^a$, $P_k^b < 1$), such that $R \geq R^*$.

In order to prove this, we assume that there exist $P_x$, $P_y$, $P_k^a$, $P_k^b$ ($0 < P_x$, $P_y$, $P_k^a$, $P_k^b < 1$), such that $R \geq R^*$.

$$\frac{\left| (P_x - P_y) \cdot (P_k^a - P_k^b) \right|}{2 \cdot P_k^b + (P_x + P_y) \cdot (P_k^a - P_k^b)} \geq \frac{\left| P_k^a - P_k^b \right|}{P_k^a + P_k^b}$$

$$\Leftrightarrow \frac{(P_x - P_y)^2 \cdot (P_k^a - P_k^b)^2}{[2 \cdot P_k^b + (P_x + P_y) \cdot (P_k^a - P_k^b)]^2} \geq \frac{(P_k^a - P_k^b)^2}{(P_k^a + P_k^b)^2}$$

$$\Leftrightarrow (P_x - P_y)^2 \cdot (P_k^a + P_k^b)^2 \geq [2 \cdot P_k^b + (P_x + P_y) \cdot (P_k^a - P_k^b)]^2$$

$$\Leftrightarrow (P_x - P_y)^2 \cdot (P_k^a + P_k^b)^2 \geq 4 \cdot P_k^{b2} + (P_x + P_y)^2 \cdot (P_k^a - P_k^b)^2$$
$$+ 4 \cdot P_k^b \cdot (P_x + P_y) \cdot (P_k^a - P_k^b)$$

Both sides divided by $(P_k^b)^2$, and let $m = \dfrac{P_k^a}{P_k^b}$

$$\Leftrightarrow (P_x - P_y)^2 \cdot (m+1)^2 \geq 4 + (P_x + P_y)^2 \cdot (m-1)^2 + 4 \cdot (P_x + P_y) \cdot (m-1)$$

$$\Leftrightarrow -4 \cdot P_x \cdot P_y \cdot m^2 + (4 \cdot P_x^2 + 4 \cdot P_y^2 - 4 \cdot P_x - 4 \cdot P_y) \cdot m - 4 \cdot P_x \cdot P_y$$
$$-4 + 4 \cdot P_x + 4 \cdot P_y \geq 0$$

Both sides divided by $(-4 \cdot P_x \cdot P_y)$

$$\Leftrightarrow m^2 + \left(\frac{1}{P_x} + \frac{1}{P_y} - P_x - P_y\right) \cdot m + \left(1 + \frac{1}{P_x \cdot P_y} - \frac{1}{P_x} - \frac{1}{P_y}\right) \le 0$$

$$\Leftrightarrow \left[m + \frac{1}{2} \cdot \left(\frac{1}{P_x} + \frac{1}{P_y} - P_x - P_y\right)\right]^2 - \frac{1}{4} \cdot \left(\frac{1}{P_x} + \frac{1}{P_y} - P_x - P_y\right)^2$$

$$+ \left(1 + \frac{1}{P_x \cdot P_y} - \frac{1}{P_x} - \frac{1}{P_y}\right) \le 0$$

Let $a = \dfrac{1}{P_x \cdot P_y}, b = P_x + P_y$

$$\Leftrightarrow \left[m + \frac{1}{2} \cdot (a \cdot b - b)\right]^2 \le \frac{1}{4} \cdot (a \cdot b - b)^2 - (1 + a - a \cdot b)$$

Let the right hand side be $\Delta$, and let $\dfrac{1}{2} \cdot (a \cdot b - b)$ be $\Phi$

$$\Leftrightarrow (m + \Phi)^2 \le \Delta \Leftrightarrow -\sqrt{\Delta} - \Phi \le m \le \sqrt{\Delta} - \Phi$$

$$m = \frac{P_k^a}{P_k^b} > 0, \therefore \sqrt{\Delta} - \Phi > 0 \Leftrightarrow \sqrt{\Delta} > \Phi \Leftrightarrow \Delta > \Phi^2$$

which is $\dfrac{1}{4} \cdot (a \cdot b - b)^2 - (1 + a - a \cdot b) > \dfrac{1}{4} \cdot (a \cdot b - b)^2$

$$\Leftrightarrow 1 + a - a \cdot b < 0$$

$$\Leftrightarrow 1 + \frac{1}{P_x \cdot P_y} - \frac{P_x + P_y}{P_x \cdot P_y} < 0 \Leftrightarrow \frac{(P_x - 1) \cdot (P_y - 1)}{P_x \cdot P_y} < 0$$

$$P_x - 1 < 0, \ P_y - 1 < 0 \Rightarrow (P_x - 1) \cdot (P_y - 1) > 0 \ \Rightarrow \frac{(P_x - 1) \cdot (P_y - 1)}{P_x \cdot P_y} > 0,$$

contradiction, end of proof.

Without loss of generality, we do not report the analysis for the special cases when $P_x$, $P_y$, $P_k^a$, $P_k^b$ can be 0 or 1.

From the above analysis, we can easily conclude that

$$\sum_{k=1}^{q} \frac{\left| \text{SUPPORT}_{ak} - \text{SUPPORT}_{bk} \right|}{\frac{1}{2}(\text{SUPPORT}_{ak} + \text{SUPPORT}_{bk})} \quad \text{is maximized when transactions}$$

generated from $S_a$ and $S_b$ are correctly separated.

# APPENDIX 2. A GENERALIZED MIXTURE REGRESSION MODEL (GLIMMIX)

Generalized linear models are regression models, where the dependent variable is specified to be distributed according to one of the members of the exponential family. Accordingly, those models deal with dependent variables that can be either continuous with normal, gamma or exponential distributions or discrete with binomial, multinomial, Poisson or negative binomial distributions. The expectation of the dependent variable is modeled as a function of a set of explanatory variables, as in standard multiple regression models (which are a special case of generalized linear models). The estimation of a single set of regression coefficients across all observations may be inadequate and potentially misleading if the observations arise from a number of unknown groups in which the coefficients differ.

The model detailed in this appendix, proposed by Wedel and DeSarbo (1995), is a general extension of the various mixture regressions developed in the past and formulated within the exponential family. It is called the GLIMMIX model, for Generalized Linear Model Mixture.

Assume the vector of observations on object $n$, $y_n$, arise from a population that is a mixture of $S$ segments in proportions $\pi_1, \ldots, \pi_s$, where we do not know in advance the segment from which a particular vector of observations arises. The probabilities $\pi_s$ are positive and sum to one. We assume that the distribution of $y_n$, given that $y_n$ comes from segment $s$, $f_s(y_{nk} \mid \theta_s)$, is one of the distributions in the exponential family or the multivariate exponential family. Conditional on segment $s$, the $y_n$ are independent. If they cannot be assumed independent across $k$ (i.e., repeated measurements on each subject or firm), a distribution within the multivariate exponential family, such as the multivariate normal or the multinomial, is appropriate. The distribution $f_s(y_{nk} \mid \theta_s)$, is characterized by parameters $\theta_{sk}$.

The means of the distribution in segment $s$ (or expectations) are denoted by $\mu_{sk}$. Some of the distributions, such as the normal, also have an associated dispersion parameter $\lambda_s$ that characterizes the variance of the observations within each segment.

We want to predict the means of the observations in each segment by using a set of explanatory variables. We specify a linear predictor $\eta_{nsk}$, which is produced by $P$ explanatory variables $X_1, \ldots, X_p (X_p = (X_{nk})$; $p=1, \ldots, P)$ and parameter vectors $\beta_s = (\beta_{sp})$ in segment $s$:

$$\eta_{nks} = \sum_{p=1}^{P} X_{nkp} \beta_{sp} \qquad (A2.1)$$

The linear predictor is thus a linear combination of the explanatory variables, and a set of coefficients that are to be estimated. The linear predictor is in turn related to the mean of the distribution, $\mu_{sk}$, through a link function $g(\cdot)$ such that in segment $s$:

$$\eta_{nsk} = g(\mu_{nsk}) \qquad (A2.2)$$

Thus for each segment, a generalized linear model is formulated with a specification of the distribution of the variable (within the exponential family), a linear predictor $\eta_{nsk}$ and a function $g(\cdot)$ that links the linear predictor to the expectation of the distribution. For each distribution there are preferred links, called canonical links. The canonical links for the normal, Poisson, binomial, gamma and inverse Gaussian distributions are the identity, log, logit, inverse and squared inverse functions, respectively. For example, for the normal distribution the identity link involves $\eta_{nsk} = \mu_{sk}$, so that by combining equations (A2.1) and (A2.2) the standard linear regression model within segments arises.

The unconditional probability density function of an observation vector $y_n$ can now be expressed in the finite mixture form:

$$f(y_n \mid \Phi) = \sum_{s=1}^{S} \pi_s f_s(y_n \mid \theta_s),$$

where the parameter vector $\Phi = (\pi_s, \theta_s)$, $\theta_s = (\beta_s, \lambda_s)$. Note that the difference with the finite mixture model is that here the mean vector of the observations (given each segment) is reparameterized in terms of regression coefficients relating the means to a set of explanatory variables. The purpose is to estimate the parameter vector $\Phi$. To do so, we maximize the likelihood equation with respect to $\Phi$. The problem can be solved using the EM algorithm.

# APPENDIX 3. DEFINITION FOR CONTRAST SETS

The data is a set of $k$-dimensional vectors where each component can take on a finite number of discrete values. The vectors are organized into $n$ mutually exclusive groups $G_1, G_2, \ldots, G_n$, with $G_i \mathbin{I} G_j = \phi, \forall_i \neq j$. The concept of an itemset can be extended to a contrast set for this type of data as follows:

**Definition A3.1**

*Let $A_1, A_2, \ldots, A_k$ be a set of k variables called attributes. Each $A_i$ can take on values from the set $\{V_{i1}, V_{i2}, \ldots, V_{im}\}$. Then a contrast set is a conjunction of attribute-value pairs defined on groups $G_1, G_2, \ldots, G_n$ with no $A_i$ occurring more than once.*

Example A3.1: sex = female ∧occupation = manager.

Similar to the definition of support for an itemset, the support of a contrast set with respect to a group $G$ is defined as follows:

**Definition A3.2**

*The support of a contrast set with respect to a group G is the percentage of examples in G where the contrast set is true.*

The goal of mining contrast set is to find all contrast sets whose support differs meaningfully across groups. Formally, we want to find those contrast sets (cset) where:

$$\exists i, j P(\text{cset} = \text{True} \,|\, G_i) \neq P(\text{cset} = \text{True} \,|\, G_j) \qquad \text{(A3.1)}$$

$$\max_{i,j} \left| \text{support}(\text{cset}, G_i) - \text{support}(\text{cset}, G_j) \right| \geq \delta \qquad \text{(A3.2)}$$

And $\delta$ is a user defined threshold called the minimum support difference. We call contrast sets where Equation (A3.1) is statistically valid significant, and contrast sets where Equation 2 is met large.

# APPENDIX 4. VARIABLES IN EXPERIMENT I

TABLE 15.    Variables in Experiment I

|  | No. | Variables | Description |
|---|---|---|---|
| Demographics | 1 | hoh_most_education | 0~5 |
| | 2 | census_region | North East, North Central, West, South |
| | 3 | household_size | 1~6 |
| | 4 | hoh_oldest_age | 1~11 |
| | 5 | household_income | 1~7 |
| | 6 | child_present | Yes, No |
| | 7 | racial_background | White, Black, Asian, Other |
| | 8 | connection_speed | Narrowband, Broadband |
| | 9 | country_of_origin | Hispanic, Non-hispanic |
| Browsing-related | 10 | sum_duration | Total time spent on the site |
| | 11 | avg_ session_duration | Average time spent per session |
| | 12 | num_session | Total number of sessions |
| | 13 | num_day | Total number of days visited |
| | 14 | num_hit | Total number of hits (pages viewed) |
| | 15 | avg_num_hit_session | Average number of hits per session |
| | 16 | Recency_visit | number of weeks since last visit (coded 1-3) |
| Purchase-related | 17 | num_purchase | Total number of purchases (shopping trips) |
| | 18 | num_product (Frequency of purchase) | Total number of products bought |
| | 19 | sum_amount (Monetary value) | Total amount of money spent |
| | 20 | avg_purchase | Average amount spent per purchase (shopping trip) |
| | 21 | avg_price | Average price for the products bought |
| | 22 | Recency_purchase | number of weeks since last purchase (coded 1-3) |
| | 23 | num_category | Total number of product categories purchased |
| Y | 24 | total_amount | Total amount of money spent on the Web site |

# BIBLIOGRAPHY

[1]   Adomavicius, G. and Tuzhilin, A., 2001, "Using Data Mining Methods to Build Customer Profiles", *IEEE Computer*, 34(2):74-82.

[2]   Aggarwal, C. C. et al., 1999, "Fast algorithms for projected clustering." In *SIGMOD 1999*.

[3]   Aggarwal, C. C. and Yu, P. S., 2000, "Finding generalized projected clusters in high dimensional spaces". In *SIGMOD 2000*.

[4]   Agrawal, R., Mannila, H., Srikant, R., Toivonen, H., and Verkamo, A. I., 1995, "Fast Discovery of Association Rules", *Advances in Know. Discovery and Data Mining*, Chapter 12, AAAI/MIT Press.

[5]   Agrawal, R. et al., 1998, "Automatic subspace clustering of high dimensional data for data mining applications". In *SIGMOD 1998*.

[6]   Allenby, G. M. and Rossi, P. E., 1999, "Marketing Models of Consumer Heterogeneity", *Journal of Econometrics,* 89:57-78.

[7]   Ansari, A., Essegaier, S., and Kohli, R., 2000, "Internet Recommendation Systems," *Journal of Marketing Research*, 37(3).

[8]   Avriel, M., 1976, *Nonlinear Programming: Analysis and Methods*, Englewood Cliffs, NJ: Prentice-Hall, Inc.

[9]   Bay, S. D. and Pazzani, M. J., 2001, "Detecting Group Differences: Mining Contrast Sets". *Data Mining and Knowledge Discovery*, 5(3):213-46.

[10]  Beil, F., Eater, M., and Xu, X., 2002, "Frequent Term-Based Text Clustering", In *Proc. 8th Int. Conf. on Knowledge Discovery and Data Mining (KDD '2002)*, Edmonton, Alberta, Canada.

[11]  Bell, D. R. and Lattin, J. M., 2000, "Looking for Loss Aversion in Scanner Panel Data: The Confounding Effect of Price Response Heterogeneity." *Marketing Science*, 19(2):185-200.

[12]  Böhning, D., 1995, "A Review of Reliable Maximum Likelihood Algorithms for Semiparametric Mixture Models," *Journal of Statistical Planning and Inference*, 47:5-28.

[13]  Bolton, R. J. and Hand, D. J., 2001, "Unsupervised Profiling Methods for Fraud Detection", *Credit Scoring and Credit Control VII*, Edinburgh, UK, Sept. 2001.

[14]  Brijs, T., Goethals, B., Swinnen, G., Vanhoof, K., and Wets, G., 2000, "A Data Mining Framework for Optimal Product Selection in Retail Supermarket Data: The Generalized PROFSET Model", *Proceedings of the sixth ACM SIGKDD international conference on Knowledge discovery and data mining*, August 20-23, 2000, Boston, MA.

[15] Chan, P., Fan, W., Prodromidis, A., and Stolfo, S., 1999, "Distributed data mining in credit card fraud detection", *IEEE Intelligent Systems*, 67-74.

[16] Chauchat, J.-H., Rakotomalala, R., Carloz, M., and Pelletier, C., 2001, "Targeting Customer Groups using Gain and Cost Matrix: a Marketing Application", *ECML/PKDD-01 Workshop on Data Mining for Marketing Applications*, 12th European Conference on Machine Learning (ECML'01) and 5th European Conference on Principles and Practice of Knowledge Discovery in Databases (PKDD'01), September, 2001, Freiburg, Germany.

[17] Chiang, W. K., Chhajed, D., and Hess, J. D., 2003, "Direct Marketing, Indirect Profits: A Strategic Analysis of Dual-Channel Supply-Chain Design", *Management Science*, 49(1):1-20.

[18] Cooke, A. D. J., Sujan, H., Sujan, M., and Weitz, B. A., 2002, "Marketing the Unfamiliar: The Role of Context and Item-Specific Information in Electronic Agent Recommendations." *Journal of Marketing Research*, 39(4):488-497.

[19] Cortes, C., Fisher, K., Pregibon, D., and Rogers, A., 2000, "HANCOCK: A Language for Extracting Signatures from Data Streams", In *Proceedings of the Sixth ACM International Conference on Knowledge Discovery and Data Mining*, 9-17, 2000.

[20] Cox, B., 2002, "Adventures in the Shipping Wars", *Jupitermedia*.

[21] Danaher, P. J., Wilson, I. W., and Davis, R. A., 2003, "A Comparison of Online and Offline Consumer Brand Loyalty." *Marketing Science*, 22(4):461-476.

[22] Delhagen, K., 2003, "Succeeding With Your 2002 To 2003 Transition," Forrester Research, FirstLook Archive.

[23] DeSarbo, W. S. and Cron W. L., 1988, "A Maximum Likelihood Methodology for Clusterwise Linear Regression," *Journal of Classification*, 5:249-282.

[24] Dillon, W. R., Kumar A., and Borrero, M. S., 1993, "Capturing Individual Differences in Paired Comparisons: An Extended BTL Model Incorporating Descriptor Variables," *Journal of Marketing Research*, 30:42-51.

[25] DMA, 2004, "Survey Studies Why Consumers Abandon Online Shopping Carts; Shipping and Handling Costs Trigger 52% of Abandonment", *The Direct Marketing Association Newsstand*, January 14, 2004.

[26] Ericsson, R., 2003, "Delve Into Data With Business Intelligence," *Windows Server System Magazine*, March 2003 Issue.

[27] Fawcett, T. and Provost, F., 1997, "Adaptive Fraud Detection", *Data Mining and Knowledge Discovery*, 1-28, 1997, Kluwer Academic Publishers.

[28] Fraley, C. and Raftery, A. E., 1998, "How many clusters? Which clustering method? – Answers via Model-Based Cluster Analysis", *Computer Journal*, 41:578-588.

[29]   Fraley, C. and Raftery, A. E., 2002, "Model-Based Clustering, Discriminant Analysis, and Density Estimation", *Journal of the American Statistical Association*, 97:611-631.

[30]   Frank, R. E., Massy, W. F., and Wind, Y., 1972, *Market Segmentation*, Englewood Cliffs, New Jersey: Prentice Hall.

[31]   Friedman, J. H., 1991, "Multivariate Adaptive Regression Splines", *Annals of Statistics*, 19(1):1-67.

[32]   Goldberg, D., Nichols, D., Oki, B., and Terry D., 1992, "Using Collaborative Filtering to Weave an Information Tapestry", *Communications of the Association for Computing Machinery*, 35.

[33]   Gordon, A. D., 1980, *Classification*, London: Chapman and Hall.

[34]   Gupta, S. and Chintagunta, P. K., 1994, "On Using Demographic Variables to Determine Segment Membership in Logit Mixture Models," *Journal of Marketing Research*, 31(February):128-136.

[35]   Hair, J. F., Anderson, R. E., Tatham, R. L., and Black, W. C., 1992, *Multivariate Data Analysis (3rd edn.)*, New York: Macmilllan.

[36]   Han, E., Karypis, G., Kumar, V., and Mobasher, B., 1997, "Clustering based on association rule hypergraphs", In *Proceedings of the SIGMOD'97 Workshop on Research Issues in Data Mining and Knowledge Discovery*, ACM.

[37]   Hartigan, J. A., 1975, *Clustering Algorithms*, New York: Wiley.

[38]   Hess, D. J., Chu, W., and Gerstner, E., 1996, "Controlling product returns in direct marketing", *Marketing Letters*, 7(4):307-317.

[39]   Hofstede, F. T., Wedel, M., and Steenkamp, J. E. M., 2002, "Identifying Spatial Segments in International Markets." *Marketing Science*, 21(2):160-177.

[40]   Imai, H. and Iri, M., 1986, "An optimal Algorithm for Approximating a Piecewise Linear Function," *Journal of Information Processing,* 9(3).

[41]   Jagadish et al., 1999, "Semantic compression and pattern extraction with fascicles". In VLDB 1999.

[42]   Jung, H., 2003, "Amazon's free shipping pressures other dot-coms," *Associated Press*, January 28, 2003.

[43]   Kamakura, W. A., Kim, B., and Lee J., 1996, "Modeling Preference and Structural Heterogeneity," *Marketing Science*, 15(2):152-172.

[44]   Kamakura, W. A. and Russell, G. J., 1989, "A Probabilistic Choice Model for Market Segmentation and Elasticity Structure," *Journal of Marketing Research*, 26 (November):379-390.

[45]   Kamakura, W. A., Wedel, M., and Agrawal, J., 1994, "Concomitant Variable Latent Class Models for Conjoint Analysis," *International Journal of Research in Marketing*, 11, 451-464.

[46] Karypis, G., Aggarwal, R., Kumar, V., and Shekhar, S., 1997, "Multilevel hypergraph partitioning: application in VLSI domain". In *Proceedings of the ACM/IEEE Design Automation Conference*, 1997, Canada.

[47] Kleinberg, J., Papadimitriou, C., and Raghavan, P., 1998, "Segmentation Problems", In *Proceedings of the 30th ACM Symposium on Theory of Computing*, pp. 473-482, New York.

[48] Linden, G., Smith B., and York, J., 2003, "Amazon.com Recommendations: Item-to-Item Collaborative Filtering". *IEEE Distributed Systems Online*, 4(1).

[49] Manchanda, P., Ansari, A., and Gupta, S., 1999, "The 'Shopping Basket': A Model for Multicategory Purchase Incidence Decisions", *Marketing Science*, 18(2):95-114.

[50] Mani, D.R., Drew, J., Betz, A., and Datta, P., 1999, "Statistics and Data Mining Techniques for Lifetime Value Modeling," *Proceedings of KDD-99*, 94-103.

[51] McDougall, D., Wyner, G., and Vazdauskas, D., 1997, "Customer valuation as a foundation for growth", *Managing Service Quality*, 7(1).

[52] Miller, P. and Franco, M. D., 2002, "The Price of Free S&H", *Catalog Age*, Oct 1, 2002.

[53] Morwitz, V. G., Greenleaf, E. A., and Johnson, E. J., 1998, "Divide and prosper: Consumers' reactions to partitioned prices", *Journal of Marketing Research*, 35(4):453.

[54] Pei, J., Zhang, X., Cho, M., Wang, H., and Yu, P., 2003, "MaPle: A Fast Algorithm for Maximal Pattern-based Clustering", *Proceedings of the Third IEEE International Conference on Data Mining*, November 19-22, 2003.

[55] Pijls, W., Potharst, R., and Kaymak, U., 2001, "Pattern-based Target Selection applied to Fund Raising", *ECML/PKDD-01 Workshop on Data Mining for Marketing Applications*, 12th European Conference on Machine Learning (ECML'01) and 5th European Conference on Principles and Practice of Knowledge Discovery in Databases (PKDD'01), September, 2001, Freiburg, Germany.

[56] Riedl, J., 2001, "Recommender systems in commerce and community." *Proceedings of the seventh ACM SIGKDD international conference on Knowledge discovery and data mining*, Pages: 15 – 15, San Francisco, California.

[57] Ross, S., 1980, *Introduction to Probability Models*, 2nd edn., New York: Academic Press.

[58] Shaffer, G. and Zhang, Z. J., 1995, "Competitive Coupon Targeting," *Marketing Science*, 14(4):395-416.

[59]   Shannon, C. E., 1948, "A mathematical theory of communication", *Bell System Technical Journal*, 27(July and October):379-423, 623-656.

[60]   Shop.org, 2003, "High Satisfaction and Improved Fulfillment Drive Successful Online Holiday Season," http://www.shop.org/press/02/121902.html.

[61]   Späth, H., 1979, "Clusterwise Linear Regression," *Computing*, 22(4):367-373.

[62]   Späth, H., 1981, "Clusterwise Linear Regression," *Computing*, 26(26):275.

[63]   Späth, H., 1982, "A Fast Algorihtm for Clusterwise Linear Regression," *Computing*, 29(2):175-181.

[64]   Steinbach, M., Karypis, G., and Kumar, V., 2000, "A comparison of document clustering techniques." In *KDD Workshop on Text Mining*, 2000.

[65]   Strehl, A. and Ghosh, J., 2000, "Value-based customer grouping from large retail data-sets," in *Proceedings of the SPIE Conference on Data Mining and Knowledge Discovery: Theory, Tools, and Technology II*, 24-25 April 2000, Orlando, Florida, USA, vol. 4057, pp. 33-42, SPIE, April 2000.

[66]   Tong, H. , Lim, K.S., 1980, "Threshold Autoregression, Limit Cycles and Cyclical Data", *Journal of the Royal Statistical Society, Series B (Methodological)*, 42(3):245-292.

[67]   Wang, K., Xu, C., and Liu, B., 1999, "Clustering Transactions Using Large Items", *Proc. 8th Int. Conf. on Information and Knowledge Management (ACM CIKM'99)*, Kansas City.

[68]   Wang, H., Yang, J., Wang, W., and Yu, P.S., 2002, "Clustering by Pattern Similarity in Large Data Sets", *Proc. ACM SIGMOD Conference*, Madison, WI, June 2002.

[69]   Wedel, M. and DeSarbo, W. S., 1994, "A Review of Latent Class Regression Models and their Applications," in *Advanced Methods for Marketing Research*, Richard P. Bagozzi (ed.), 353-388.

[70]   Wedel, M. and DeSarbo, W. S., 1995, "A Mixture Likelihood Approach for Generalized Linear Models," *Journal of Classification*, 12(1):1-35.

[71]   Wedel, M. and Kamakura, W., 1998, *Market Segmentation: Conceptual and Methodological Foundations*, International Series in Quantitative Marketing, Kluwer Academic Publisher, Boston, MA.

[72]   Wedel, M., Kamakura, W. A., DeSarbo, W. S., and Hofstede, F., 1995, "Implications for Asymmetry, Nonproportionality and Heterogeneous in Brand Switching from Piece-Wise Exponential Hazard Models," *Journal of Marketing Research*, 32:457-462.

[73]   Weigend, A. S., Mangeas, M., and Srivastava, A. N., 1995, "Nonlinear gated experts for time series: discovering regimes and avoiding overfitting", *International Journal of Neural Systems,* 6:373-399.

[74]  Yang, Y., Guan, X., and You, J., 2002, "CLOPE: A Fast and Effective Clustering Algorithm for Transactional Data", *SIGKDD '02*, July 23-26, 2002, Edmonton, Alberta, Canada.

[75]  Yang, Y. and Padmanabhan, B., 2003, "Segmenting Customer Transactions Using a Pattern-Based Clustering Approach", In *Proceedings of the Third IEEE International Conference on Data Mining (ICDM2003)*, Melbourne, Florida, November 19-22, 2003.

[76]  Zamir, O., Etzioni, O., 1998, "Web Document Clustering: A Feasability Demonstration", *Proc. ACM SIGIR 1998*, pp. 46-54.

# Name Index

# SUBJECT INDEX

Printed in the United States
67794LVS00003B/9